This book is dedicated to my mother

Virginia P. Lonegren,

who taught me to dowse
over 25 years ago.

The Pendulum Kit

Sig Lonegren

A FIRESIDE BOOK
PUBLISHED BY SIMON & SCHUSTER INC.
NEW YORK   LONDON   TORONTO   SYDNEY   TOKYO

FIRESIDE
Simon & Schuster Building
Rockefeller Center
1230 Avenue of the Americas
New York, New York 10020

Copyright © Eddison Sadd Editions 1990
Text copyright © Sig Lonegren 1990

Designed by Nigel Partridge

3   5   7   9   10   8   6   4

ISBN 0-671-69140-6

AN EDDISON · SADD EDITION
Edited, designed and produced by
Eddison Sadd Editions Limited
St Chad's Court, 146B King's Cross Road,
London WC1X 9DH

Phototypeset by Bookworm Typesetting, Manchester, England
Origination by Columbia Offset, Singapore
Printed and bound in Hong Kong

CONTENTS

INTRODUCTION

Dowsing is a scientific art. It is a tool that can be used to bridge the gap between the analytical and the intuitive sides of our being. Many people today are looking for ways to redress the balance; to use their intuition more. Dowsing with a pendulum is an easy and natural solution. Let me explain what I mean by dowsing. Interpreting the movements of a swinging pendulum to find answers to questions is called dowsing. This means intuitively searching, or divining, as some people say, for a 'response' from the pendulum.

I first began to dowse over twenty-five years ago when my Mother taught me how to find underground water pipes in our front lawn with some bent coat-hangers (L rods, also called angle rods (page 103)). Since then I've worked mostly in the area of dowsing called the Earth Mysteries, obtaining a Masters Degree in Sacred Space, becoming a Trustee of the American Society of Dowsers (ASD) and heading their Dowsing School, writing a book called *Spiritual Dowsing*, and working with OakDragon, an organization in Britain that runs nine-day wholistic outdoor educational camps in various aspects of the Earth Mysteries.

In the last fifteen years there has been an explosion of possible uses for dowsing. We've come a long way from our recent roots where drinking water was the only thing to dowse for. Now there are a good number of dowsing books on the market. Some are too advanced for those just beginning to dowse. Others are poorly written, or focus solely on water well dowsing. This book is written for people who are just waking up to the possibilities of this ancient art, and who want to sample the various kinds of dowsing that are available today.

   This book assumes that you've never dowsed before, and is full of exercises designed to help you become a proficient dowser. This kit comes with its own pendulum (one of the basic dowsing tools). If you are the second or third reader of this book, and the pendulum has been kept by the first reader, you can easily make a pendulum for yourself. You can use a foot (30 cm) of thread tied to the weight you have chosen – something evenly balanced like a heavy ring or a hexagonal nut. If you do not have a pendulum now, please make one before you begin the first chapter. There are sections on how to use the enclosed pendulum; how dowsing might work; lots of charts to practice over, including some new ways of using dowsing together with astrology to find out more about yourself; how to make and use other dowsing tools; a discussion about dowsing and science, and a good reference section that can guide you to other books and dowsing related organizations.

   Please try to do *all* of these exercises *as* you read the book. Don't say to yourself, 'I'll read the book first, and do the exercises later.' If you do that, you'll miss the whole point. By the end of this book, if you have done the exercises, you will have a new way to consciously bring your intuition into the practical decision-making process. Welcome to a wonderful new/old world.

SIG LONEGREN

20 April 1989
Full Moon

CHAPTER 1

WHAT IS DOWSING?

I t was one of those picture book Vermont sunny days when the lawn is greener than green and a few beautiful white clouds, like big balls of cotton, framed Stannard Mountain to the east. We were sitting out on our front lawn just enjoying the day with some friends. For some reason my wife, Kathy, had been playing with her engagement ring, that had been my grandmother's, and suddenly she realized that she had lost it. Where to look? We divided up the lawn into small squares and began to frantically paw through the grass trying to feel the ring with our fingers.

Suddenly, I remembered that I had my pendulum in my pocket. I use what's called (rather unfortunately) a bullet pendulum – it's a steel weight, about the thickness of a writing pen, about 1¼ inches long (3 cm), and pointed at one end. Attached to the other end is about 6 inches (15 cm) of one of those chains that you find connected to plugs in old sinks.

As I held the chain in my hand with the weight dangling below my fingers, all kinds of thoughts were rushing through my mind, 'This ring was Nana's, and now it's important to Kathy ... The rock alone is worth a good piece of change ... Maybe it's lost forever ... Wait a minute! This is really important to me. Focus in. In what direction is Kathy's engagement ring?'

The pendulum started swinging back and forth, pointing in line slightly to my left. 'Is it in front of me?' My pendulum swung into a clockwise direction, which for me means *yes*. The hair on the back of my neck began to tingle. This is my body's way of telling me that I'm on the right track.

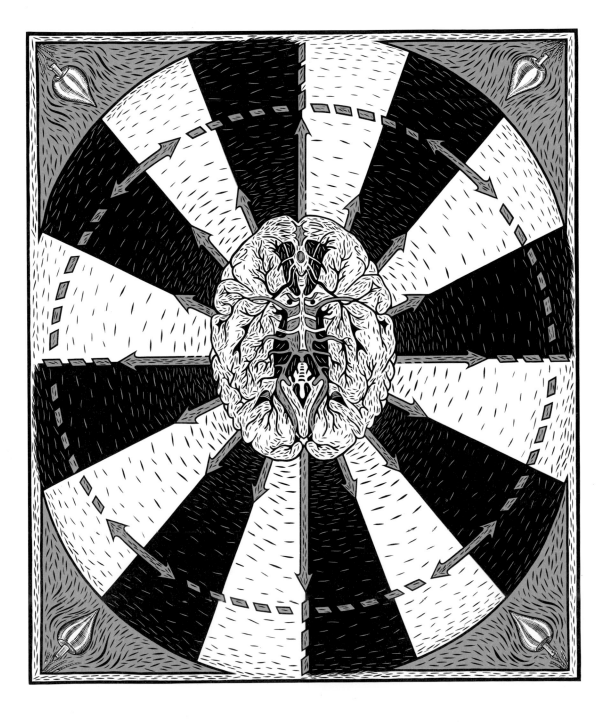

I made a mental note of the direction of that line, and moved about a yard to the left and slightly forward. Again I asked, 'In what direction is Kathy's engagement ring?' This time, the pendulum started to oscillate back and forth, pointing almost right in front of me. In my mind, I could 'see' the first line my pendulum had showed me. Then I noted the direction it was now indicating. The ring should be where the two lines crossed. I reached out my hand to that point on the lawn, and grasped at the blades of grass. I felt the ring between my fingers. How had I done this? How could a swinging steel pendulum indicate to me the position of a valued mislaid object? What is this phenomenon called dowsing and how does it work?

Let me begin by saying that in addition to being a fine tool for finding lost objects, dowsing is a way of balancing the rational aspect of our being with our intuitive. It is a tool for exploring the unconscious, a way of finding answers to questions that cannot be answered by the rational thought process or through the use of scientific methodology. And yet, the rational thought process is an integral part of the dowsing process!

So let's get into this business of dowsing, or divining, as some people call it. First of all, there is no difference between the word 'dowsing' and 'divining'. They mean the same thing. Both the British and the American Society of Dowsers are dedicated to exploring the entire spectrum of dowsing/divining possibilities. In this book, I have used 'dowsing' as it is the word most often employed to describe the method of using a pendulum (or other device). You can just as easily insert the word 'divining'.

We'll start dowsing immediately by learning two pendulum signals, or answers (*yes* and *no*), that your intuition can use to communicate with you. In trying to explore what this phenomenon of dowsing is all about, we'll look at the issues of left brain *versus* right brain, and ways of 'knowing' with a discussion about an early Christian heretical group called the Gnostics, whose philosophy can help us to better understand the dowsing process. I believe that intuition and dowsing are one and the same, and dowsing will certainly cause you to exercise your intuitive faculties. We'll look at several possible ways of explaining dowsing, including an analogy with radar and comparison with the hologram.

THE EXERCISES

Throughout this book we will be doing dowsing exercises.

These exercises will be printed in italics, like this sentence, to remind you that you need to do more than just read that passage.

To really get anything out of this book requires your active participation. You can't learn how to dowse by just reading about it, you actually have to dowse. This package comes with a dowsing tool called a pendulum, a conical brass weight on the end of a flexible cord.

Let's get right into the first dowsing exercise, and use this amazing little tool. We want to begin by finding out three different responses that can be made. The first is the *search position*. This is the, 'I'm ready to go' position.

Hold your hand with your thumb and forefinger pointing down, and the cord of the pendulum between them. Allow about 2 inches (5 cm) of cord between your hand and the brass weight. You can rest your elbow on a table if you feel this is more comfortable.

Hold your pendulum like this.

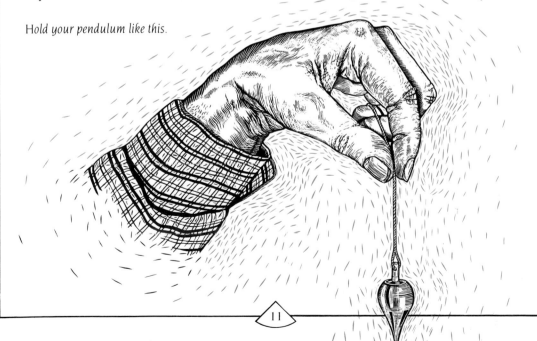

The *search position* is the place from which you will begin all of the other dowsing operations that you will learn in this book. In the use of the pendulum, there are no universal reactions. Not everybody's *search position* is the same. Usually, it is one of two reactions. Either there is no movement at all (the pendulum just hangs there as if the weight were dead), or goes back and forth, directly towards you and then away. Both of these are acceptable search positions. For several years, I co-headed the annual dowsing school for the American Society of Dowsers with Edward Jastram. Ed's search position was dead still, mine was, and still is, back and forth. Here's your first exercise.

Hold your pendulum as shown in the illustration. Say to your pendulum, 'Show me my search position. I *want to see my* search position.'
  The best thing about this is that your first attempt at dowsing will be totally successful, even if your pendulum doesn't move at all!

Now for *yes*. Again, there is no universal *yes* response; however, most dowsers find that it is one of two reactions. If the search position is totally still, some dowsers find that their *yes* response is back and forth — as when you nod your head, *yes*. Many dowsers find that their *yes* is a clockwise circle. Either response is fine.

Hold your pendulum in your search position, *and ask the following question, 'In the Spring, when the grass first comes up, is it green?' Of course, you know that the answer to this question is yes, so watch your pendulum closely for any deviation from the* search position. *You might also try, 'Show me yes, show me yes.'*
  If your pendulum doesn't seem to want to move of its own accord, make it move! I recommend that you make it go in a clockwise direction. As you do, say to yourself (or out loud if you're not too self-conscious), 'This is yes, this is positive, this is yang, this is yes.'

Now let's find *no*. If your *yes* response was back and forth, perhaps you will find that your *no* is from side to side — just like you move your head to indicate no. On the other hand, if your *yes* was clockwise, perhaps you will find that your *no* response is counterclockwise. Try to find your *no* response by working through the next exercise.

Hold your pendulum in your search position, and ask the following question, 'Is snow green?' Again, you know the answer, so watch your pendulum for any deviation from the search position that isn't your yes response. This is your no response.

So it didn't work. That's ok. Lots of beginners have a hard time getting the pendulum to work on its own (at least that's the feeling one has when it works for the first time). So I suggest that you make it move counterclockwise, and say to yourself, 'This is no, this is receptive, this is yin, this is no.'

If you do these exercises several times a day for the next week, your pendulum dowsing skills will be established. What is happening is that you are communicating with your unconscious, and setting up a code. It really doesn't matter what the code is, the important thing is that you have one, up to this point, with three different recognizable signals for *search*, *yes* and *no*. Promise yourself you will do these three exercises daily this week. It will really help you to develop as a dowser.

LEFT BRAIN AND RIGHT BRAIN

We live in a world today that emphasizes rational thought. When we went to school, we struggled with questions like, 'What were the five steps leading up to the American Civil War?', or, 'If the radius of a circle is four, what is the circumference?' While the question of who discovered Mexico was important, no one seemed interested in how the Aztec people felt when they realized what Cortez and his conquistadors were up to. We tend to see history as a series of outcomes and events. We have been taught to be analytical, to follow orders, and to regurgitate the 'right' answer, but it can be argued that few teachers seemed interested in strengthening our intuitive, feeling side.

Over the past ten or fifteen years there has been a lot written about the left and right sides of the brain. The left brain seems to govern the right side of our body, and our analytical, or linear, capabilities. If you have a stroke, and your right side is paralyzed, you might not be able to speak — speech is a linear activity, the subject has to come before the verb, which in turn comes before the direct object. The right brain governs the left side of our body, and seems to be the seat of more subjective, intuitive abilities as well as the ability to function wholistically. It is this aspect of our being that recognizes other people. We don't look at someone's nose, their lips, eyes, and hair and then say, 'Oh, that's you Jack!' It isn't a linear function, we take the person's face in all at once, and know who it is. It is also said that the right side of our brain governs our intuitive capabilities. While recent research has shown that it is simplistic to state that the left brain is rational and the right brain is intuitive, for the purposes of this book, it continues to be a useful metaphor.

Our rational side is well fed – over fed; however, for most of us, our intuitive, subjective side is starving. Our schools, our jobs, and our governments just don't seem to value this half of our being. It's like walking through life with one eye closed. Many people are awakening to the realization that for complete fulfilment they must begin to tap into the intuitive, subjective half of their being. Dowsing is a skill that can be very helpful here.

If one 'knows' something in today's modern world. it means that anyone else can also know it by using their own five senses (or have a needle move on an electronic instrument). To know something is to be able to prove it by using the scientific method. The verb 'to know' comes to us through Middle English; as *knowen*, which can be traced back to the Latin, *gnoscere* – to know.

But *gnoscere* also has another meaning, one that was lost, or at least suppressed, along the way. The early group of Christian heretics called the Gnostics viewed many aspects of life in ways that angered and threatened members of the early Church. Among their ideas was the view that women were equal to men and indeed, women officiated at Gnostic gatherings. This was not very popular with the Church Fathers. Early Church history is called 'patristics', from the Latin, *'pater'* which means father. It would seem that there was no room for the feminine (intuitive) energy of women in early Church hierarchy.

Gnostics intended to know, or, you could say to *gnow*, the spiritual realms directly and personally. While they were open to the teachings of many, ultimately, they felt spiritual responsibility lay within each individual. Gnostics could not accept that one person in Rome could be the ultimate arbiter of what was spiritually valid for everyone. This was because they had directly experienced the intangible spiritual realms themselves, and could therefore decide or *gnow* reality for themselves. They claimed the sole right for themselves to *gnow* what was true and what wasn't.

When one *intuitively knows* something, it is invariably not provable by any rational process. When one *knows* that God exists, one cannot smell, taste, see, hear or touch God; that realization does not come through the five physical senses. *Knowing* in this way speaks to the intuitive side of our being, not the rational. Dowsing, then, is a way of *intuitively knowing*.

Dowsing, as has been said before, is also a scientific art. Perhaps you've heard of dowsing, or divining, in terms of looking for water, and indeed this continues to be one of the most important aspects of this ancient form of divination. To be good at dowsing, one must be both good at science (read: rational), *and* at art (read: intuitive). Firstly, you must be able to ask the right question, for example, if some friends need a new well, you can't just go to their house and ask, 'Where's the nearest water?'

You might detect water that is 700 feet (213 m) down, yields 2 fluid ounces (59 ml) an hour, tastes like sulphur, and goes dry every year from April to September. So instead of, 'Where's the nearest water?', the question needs to be something like, 'I have to dig this well myself, so where's the nearest good potable (drinkable) water, less than 20 feet (6 m) down, with a year 'round flow of at least 5 gallons (19 l) a minute?' This is the right question. This is the 'scientific' part of the art of dowsing – asking the right question.

Then comes the intuitive part, that portion of your brain that can apprehend things immediately without reasoning. Somehow, you have to temporarily shut down the left side of your brain, the analytical side, and open up the intuitive side – so you can *gnow* the answer. The dowsing tool can then give you the best answer, and it is truly amazing how often, in the hands of a competent dowser, it does work. A good water witch, as they are called by some dowsers, is successful between 85 and 90 percent of the time!

Why do I place so much importance on intuition? I thought that we lived in a world where our rational mind could solve all of our problems. Many people believe that this is so, but interestingly enough, this isn't how it seems to work. From Archimedes suddenly discovering specific gravity while sitting in the bath-tub, and jumping up shouting, 'Eureka! (I've got it!)' to the most successful, modern businessmen who, studies have shown, go with their hunches, intuition has played an important part in the development of rational, linear-thinking, western man.

Albert Einstein is another good example. He thought in creative spurts. I live in a house that used to belong to Luther Eisenheart, who was one of Einstein's mathematicians at Princeton University. Incidentally, Einstein did not achieve high results for mathematics in elementary school; he thought in creative jumps. It was the task of Professor Eisenheart to complete the formulas and equations that connected Einstein's creative leaps.

Dowsing can also be seen as apparently irrational leaps. It gives answers to questions that can't be (or at least take a long time to be) found through rational means. The water dowser can't see, touch, smell, hear, or taste an underground vein of water, and yet, it can be found. Dowsing takes us beyond our rational mind, yet perhaps, most importantly, dowsing doesn't require that you reject rational thought. It is not either a rational or an intuitive issue. Dowsing requires both abilities. You have to ask the right question (left brain) and then let your intuitive side (right brain) search for the answer. And, it is possible to dowse for anything that you can think of; you're only limited by your imagination. In addition to underground veins of water, people today dowse for oil, minerals, treasure, missing persons, health, earth energies, and all kinds of other targets, both tangible and intangible.

Many times, instead of actual physical targets, people dowse to get the answer to *yes* or *no* questions – from, 'Is this pear ripe?', to, 'Is this a positive direction for me in my life right now?' It is this questioning aspect of dowsing that we will focus on in this book – how we can get answers to questions that are of particular relevance and importance in our own lives.

HOW DOES IT WORK?

This is the question I know you must be dying to ask. The honest answer is that we really don't know, but there are a few theories. The first one has to do with radar. When looking for an underground vein of water, perhaps, like radar, the dowser sends out some kind of signal that searches for the target. When it finds the target, the signal bounces back to the dowser and makes the tool move. Another possibility is that perhaps the vein of water itself sends out some kind of signal which is picked up by the dowser.

But how can radar or emanations from beneath the earth explain how dowsing can give you the answer to *yes* or *no* questions like, 'Is this a positive direction for me in my life right now?' How can the water dowser find a specific vein of water that will produce over 5 gallons (19 l) per minute, and will also run all year round? Radar, at least as we presently understand it, can't account for this. Radar can monitor and detect existing objects but can't look into the future or into the past. It can't tell how much water the vein has produced in the past, or what its capacity will be in the future. So, either radar is not the way dowsing operates, or it is only one of several ways that dowsing can work.

One possible explanation for the question of how dowsing might work, utilizes the hologram. In 1981, Rupert Sheldrake, a London based bio-chemist, wrote a book called *A New Science Of Life*. In it, he proposed an old/new way of looking at reality. Instead of a three-dimensional or linear view of reality, he had a vision that had the hologram at its foundation. This view gave me a totally different perspective, concerning the question, 'What is reality?'.

Unlike a normal photographic negative of, say, a banana, a holographic negative looks like.someone threw a handful of pebbles into a calm pond – a series of concentric interference patterns. If you tear off a corner of a photographic negative, and then print it, you'll only see a portion of the picture, let's say of a banana; however, if you tear off a part of a holographic negative, and then put coherent light (a laser beam) through it, you'll still see the whole banana – perhaps not quite so sharply, but still, the whole thing.

Perhaps the entire universe is like a holographic negative, and we are each tiny pieces of that negative. We have it all inside us. If God is within, and God is omniscient (all knowing/*gnowing*), then of course we can find the answer to the question, 'Does this vein of water run all year 'round?'

If we are part of the hologram of the entire universe, then the answers can be found by going within ourselves. Many people who meditate will tell you that this makes sense. According to the holographic model, somewhere within our beings is that tiny piece of the hologram that has the answer to any question we might ask. Others call it the still small voice.

The holographic model therefore, suggests that dowsing answers come from inside each dowser. Radar, on the other hand, is external. Some signal from inside us goes out, and when it's found the target, it bounces back to us. Another possible explanation is that dowsing tunes us in to a 'big library in the sky', similar to the Akashic Record of the Hindus, a place where all that has ever been is recorded. That's outside again.

The pendulum is a tool that can open us up to our intuitive side. In order for it to work, we must use both the rational and intuitive aspects of ourselves. The Gnostics were able to use this intuitive way of gnowing, and dowsing can make it available to us today. So how does dowsing work? The actual answer is probably found in all of the above explanations. We really don't know. At different times, and for a variety of reasons, dowsing seems to operate in diverse ways and on contrasting levels. We have compared the action of dowsing with some other mediums, including radar and a hologram, but from a pragmatic point of view, ultimately it doesn't matter how dowsing works; the main thing is that it does – at least most of the time. This does not sound very reliable, but it's important to keep in mind that our rational side isn't always 100 percent accurate. However, working together, the rational and the intuitive can greatly increase our chances of finding the best answer. The purpose of this little book is to make our intuition, our sense of *gnowing* (intuitively knowing) work more often than it does now.

Let's begin by doing those simple pendulum exercises again. Hold the pendulum between your thumb and forefinger and say, 'Show me my search position.'

Once you have that say, 'Show me yes.' Watch your pendulum respond, 'This is yes, this is positive, this is yang, this is yes.'

And now try, 'Show me no.' Then, 'This is no, this is receptive, this is yin, this is no.'

Congratulations, you're on your way to becoming a dowser!

Please remember to keep up these exercises. Sometimes you'll be asked to put down this book and get some things together for another exercise. If at all possible do the exercises *as* you read this book. Later chapters will make more sense to you if you do the exercises as you go along.

CHAPTER 2

GETTING STARTED WITH YOUR PENDULUM

T here is no right way for everyone to dowse, there's only a right way for you, and as you work at your dowsing, you'll discover what works best *for you*. There are many different suggestions throughout this book, and I trust that you will try them all, but in the end, only you can decide the dowsing style that suits you. For example, which hand do you hold your pendulum in? Notice that I have never suggested which hand to hold it in before, but you naturally *gnew* (intuitively knew) which was the best one. Continue using the hand you started with. Remember to relax as you go through the exercises with your pendulum. Don't try too hard to achieve what you think must be the correct response.

The next pendulum response that we'll work on is the one that tells us 'maybe' or that we have asked the wrong question. Once you have learned the *yes*, *no*, and *maybe* responses, it is useful to play the childrens' game known as 'Twenty Questions', or 'Animal, Vegetable, Mineral' to practice your skill at achieving the responses.

In working on any dowsing operation, 'tuning in' is one of the most important skills a dowser can develop. While there's no universally correct way of tuning in, I offer a process that can assist you in focusing on the dowsing issue at hand. This is followed by some practical dowsing exercises with coins, and an initial discussion of why dowsing doesn't always work. The pendulum can also show you direction. This chapter will end with some exercises using the leading edge concept and a method of triangulation used to locate a particular point.

THE MAYBE RESPONSE

Up to this point, you have been working on the *search position*, *yes*, and *no* responses. Now let's work for a fourth one. It's the, 'Your line of questioning is going in the wrong direction' response, or, 'That just doesn't make any sense', or, to put it most simply, the *maybe/wrong question* response. Not every question you ask will make sense in terms of what you are ultimately trying to find out. This response will let you know if you're on the wrong track.

Hold your pendulum in the search position. *Most dowsers find that the* maybe/wrong question *response is halfway between back and forth, and side to side – at a forty-five degree angle. Give it a try.*

   Ask your pendulum, 'Show me my maybe/wrong question *response.' If your pendulum doesn't seem to want to move, make it go back and forth at forty-five degrees, or from 10:30 to 4:30 on the face of a clock, or from 1:30 to 7:30.*

Most people find that the maybe/wrong question *response follows either one of the two paths that cross in the center at forty-five degrees to the* search position. *See diagram* ABOVE RIGHT.

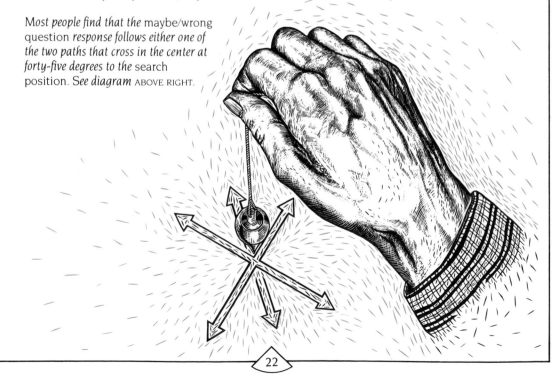

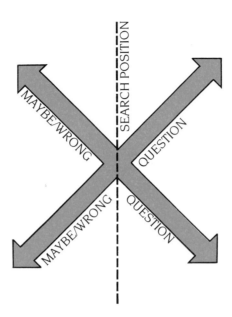

You now have four different pendulum responses. With these basic movements you can obtain an answer to almost any question that you can imagine. Using the technique of the old game, Twenty Questions (Is it Animal? Mineral? Vegetable? Is it bigger than a bread box? Is it in our kitchen? The living room? etc.), you can use dowsing to find out the answer to just about anything.

There are pitfalls, however, and the difference between a beginner and an experienced, competent dowser is that the beginner invariably falls into those pits. As I've said before, asking the right question is critical. As you phrase the question, try to make sure that it can be taken only one way. Your unconscious takes things very literally (remember my previous example, 'Where's the closest water?'), so think it through, and phrase the question so that it is as clear as possible. If you don't begin with the right question, you won't get the right answer. It's as simple as that.

TUNING IN

The next step is tuning in. It's like turning on the radio and tuning in to the correct frequency. I use four preparatory steps, or questions, to tune in. I state what I want to do, and hope to get a *yes*. Then I ask three simple but important questions: 'Can I?' 'May I?' 'Am I ready?'

'Can I?' has to do with whether I have the dowsing skills to get the correct answer to my question. (You probably remember that old one from school, 'Teacher, can I go to the bathroom?' 'Of course you can, but you *may* not go until you finish your test.') At this moment you might well have the skills necessary to find a ring that your friend has lost somewhere in the room, but perhaps you can't yet dowse something in the future, also called dowsing in time. The question, 'Can I?' will let you know if you have the necessary skill level.

'May I?' has to do with permission. This may not seem very relevant now, but there are some things that accomplished dowsers get involved with that can get the novice into all sorts of difficulties. Dabbling with the occult or using the pendulum to seek answers for unexplained phenomena are some of the things that experienced, competent dowsers can deal with, but that can lead a beginner astray. It is wise to seek permission before embarking on this kind of questioning.

There might also be karmic implications. Karma has to do with the weighing out of good deeds versus bad deeds, and lessons to be learned as a result. You might feel tempted to dowse the daily lottery numbers or the horses, but using your dowsing/intuitive skills to maximize any benefit on the physical level might have an adverse effect, 'karmically', on other levels. 'May I?' can help to prevent you from straying into areas that are not going to be of positive use to you.

So, who gives you the permission when you ask, 'May I?' There are several possible answers to this one, and all are about as tenuous as the answer to the question, 'Where do dowsing answers come from?' My own feeling is that we have a spirit guide who keeps an eye on us, something similar to the higher self (the utterly trustworthy mother/father) in the Huna, a Hawaiian spiritual path, or perhaps Jung's concept of the Self. In any event, it seems that some more evolved power with our best interests at heart is out there looking after us, and the question, 'May I?' gives that power or force the chance to speak to us directly, to help us to maintain a sensible course of action.

Asking permission is an essential condition when using a pendulum in healing, another area where dowsing is proving to be an important tool. There's nothing more irritating or intrusive than to go to a dowsing conference and to have someone rush over to you and start dowsing your aura, or telling you what's wrong with you, before asking if it is all right to do so. This psychic invasion of another's privacy just isn't the right thing to do. Such people have learned something new, and they're bursting to show others how much they know (notice I didn't say *gnow* as they haven't learnt to be intuitive). Permission is important.

So we have, 'This is what I want to do. Can I? May I?' The final tuning-in question is, 'Am I ready?' Have I done everything that is necessary to get an appropriate answer? Is there something else that I need to do to tune in? It is at this point, assuming that you have received positive responses so far, that you actually ask the question.

But, what if you get a *no* to any of these questions? The answer is simple. If you trust this process, and you get a *no*, but continue on anyway, you cannot trust the answer. So you have to go back to the beginning. Wait a minute or two, and try asking the question again, in a slightly different way. If you still get a *no* to one of the four tuning-in steps, try dowsing a totally different question about another topic. Go back to your original question later.

One of the most meaningful ways that you can use dowsing as you read this book, is to question any process or idea that you might read on these pages. One of the most important books I read as I prepared to become a teacher in the late 1960s was *Teaching as a Subversive Activity* by Neil Postman and Charles Weingartner. The subversive activity that the title refers to is getting children in elementary and secondary schools to think for themselves. This is truly subversive when you stop to think that the major objectives of many schools today are to teach children to sit in straight rows, to keep quiet, and to give teachers the answers they want to hear. In that kind of atmosphere, thinking is truly a subversive activity.

In order to think for yourself, you must first be able to listen to others, and then make up your own mind as to the validity of what you have heard. This is a truly gnostic concept. I am open to what you have to say, but ultimately I'll make up my own mind, thank you. With this in mind, Postman and Weingartner entitled their first chapter 'Crap Detecting.' This is one of the ways that I suggest you use your pendulum as you read this book.

Let's try an exercise. Determine for yourself the relevance of these tuning-in steps. The question here is, 'Are Sig's four tuning-in steps useful for me to use at this point?'

Hold your pendulum in your search position.

Say that you want to ask a question about these four steps, 'This is what I want to do. I want to find out if these four steps are useful to me now.'

'Can I?' Do I have enough dowsing skills to do this?

'May I?' Do I have permission? Again, perhaps an irrelevant question here, but it's part of the process.

'Am I ready?'

(Assuming that you received yes each time.) 'Are Sig's four tuning-in steps useful for me to use at this point?'

So what was your answer? I trust that most readers got *yes* all the way through. Many dowsers around the world use some tuning-in process similar to this. If, by some odd chance, you got a *no* somewhere in that exercise, try it again when you get farther into this book. Notice that the question used the words 'at this point.' Perhaps you don't need this tuning-in process right now. Maybe you are confident that your responses are accurate at this stage.

THE THREE COINS EXERCISE

Now for your first real dowsing exercises. You will need three coins – two of identical denomination (and even date if possible), and a third coin of a different denomination.

Place two similar coins about a palm-width apart, and hold your pendulum in your search position halfway between the two coins. Deliberately start oscillating your pendulum back and forth between the two coins. Start with just a little oscillation, and watch it build up to

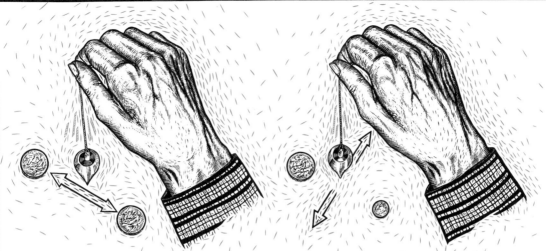

Notice how your pendulum seems to be equally drawn to each of the similar coins, LEFT. With dissimilar coins, RIGHT, the pendulum is repelled, and oscillates midway between the two coins.

longer and longer swings. It's almost as if the tip of the pendulum is trying to reach out to each coin. You can feel the similarity of the two coins, and you can feel the attraction between the pendulum and each of the coins.

Now put the different coin in the place of one of the similar coins. Instead of an obvious pulling towards the two coins, your pendulum will either go in a circle (either way), or side to side between the two coins, or perhaps some other motion, but there won't be the same pull, or attraction, that there was between the two similar coins.

Experiment with this reaction a bit. Move the coins around in different patterns. How does your pendulum react when you place three similar coins in a triangle — each coin being a palm-width from the other two?

You might like to try the above exercise with three coins of the same denomination, with two displaying the same date. Put them all on the table, date face down, and mix them up. Take any two, without looking at the date, and dowse to see if they're similar or different.

THE COIN TOSS EXERCISE

You'll need a friend to help you with this one. This is actually somewhat subversive, as it's a good way to get someone else interested in dowsing.

You'll need a good-sized coin, your pendulum, a pen or pencil, and a piece of paper to record your results

Say to yourself that you want to dowse to see if a flipped coin is heads or tails. 'Can I? May I? Am I ready?'

Put the coin on the table heads up, and hold your pendulum over it. It will go from the search position into your yes response. Now turn the coin over, and see how your pendulum goes into a no response. (These responses could be reversed – it doesn't matter.)

Have your friend flip the coin and record heads or tails on the paper. As they record the answer, you ask your pendulum if it is heads or tails. If it is heads, your pendulum will go into the yes response; if tails, it will go into your no response. Call out your answer to your friend who will also write down your responses. Do this ten times. Ask your friend not to indicate how you are doing until the end.

So how did you do? You had a fifty-fifty chance of being right each time, so if there is nothing to dowsing, the odds say that you will have got five of the ten correct. If you got more than five, hurray! If you got less than five that is also statistically significant.

The real point here has to do with mistakes. Dowsers – especially beginners – make lots of mistakes. It's like riding a bicycle. Nobody ever learned to ride without falling off. It's part of the process. The important thing for the rider to do is to get back up on that bicycle right away, and to try it again. Also, one of the best definitions of being human is that we are imperfect. (If we knew that we were perfect, we wouldn't be here on this planet.) So, again, in the long run, I believe that no dowser is ever 100 percent accurate.

So, if you didn't do so well on the coin flip exercise, try it again. Only this time, go a bit more slowly. Take your time. Achieving a successful dowsing technique, like any other skill, takes time. Persevere! You could even ask your coin-tossing friend to try the pendulum!

I've been working on this exercise with a friend of mine, Dr. Eleanor Ott. She was one of my field faculty when I did my Masters work in Sacred Space in the late 1970s at Goddard College. We extended the coin toss to include the past and the future. One of us would flip the coin ten times, recording each flip, then the other would dowse all ten. For the future, one dowses the result *before* the other flips the coin. This is a simple exercise, but it is a good way to work on your basic dowsing techniques, and also, if you do well, it will build your confidence.

THE INFLUENCE OF EMOTION

Not every dowser does well at all kinds of dowsing. Just because you are a good dowser in the area of health, it doesn't necessarily mean that you are also a good water dowser. Dowsing for health and for water take different skills. So maybe the coin toss isn't for you. But what can you do to improve the odds? There are two things you can try. First of all, while you probably don't have too much emotional investment in the result of any given coin flip, many dowsers 'lose it' in the brief time between when they ask the question and when the pendulum shows the answer. By 'lose it' I mean some dowsers lose their focus at this point, and think about the answer, or try to guess. If you do that, you can't trust the answer. Flip that coin over again.

Perhaps a different illustration might demonstrate this point more clearly. Let's say, for example, that your brother is very ill, and you suspect he may have cancer. You ask his permission to dowse him, and go through the, 'This is what I want to do, Can I, May I, Am I ready?' Then the fateful question, 'Does my brother have cancer?'

Of course you want the answer to be *no*. Perhaps, as you are waiting for the answer at that fateful point, you would subconsciously be saying to yourself, 'I hope the answer's *no*, dear God, let the answer be *no*.'

With this situation, *no* is the answer that I guarantee you will get. Dowsing answers come through our unconscious, and our unconscious is so anxious to please, that it will give us any answer that it thinks we want to hear.

When it involves someone you know and love, any form of divination is always difficult. I read tarot cards, and I've found that it is always easier to read the cards for a total stranger than it is for a friend.

The point here is that what you really want is the truth. When you asked, 'Does my brother have cancer?' you wanted, I assume, the truth. So how can you detach your emotional need for a certain answer from the actual answer? The Bible gives us a clue when it says, 'Unless ye be as a child ye shall not enter the kingdom of heaven.' After you ask the question, you need to close down your left brain with all of its thoughts and needs that, at that point, do nothing but cause confusion. So, after asking the question, try to adopt an attitude of a child's innocent expectancy and say to yourself, 'I wonder what the answer's going to be, I wonder what the answer's going to be?' Say this over and over until your pendulum shows you a response. If you're wondering what the answer is going to be, you don't have time to suggest to your unconscious what specific answer you want. It is very easy to influence the pendulum with your own subjective desire for a specific answer.

Obviously, you won't be as emotionally involved with the coin flips exercise as you would with the issue of whether or not your brother has cancer, but perhaps, after finding that the last four flips you dowsed 'heads', your left brain says, 'so it must be time for 'tails'.'

Each coin toss has a fifty-fifty chance of being heads. A small voice is leading you astray. It's the same situation – your expectation is deliberately influencing the outcome.

If you find yourself having these kinds of thoughts, try having your friend flip the coin, and as you dowse it, say to yourself, 'I wonder what the answer is going to be, I wonder what the answer is going to be?' Another method of improving the accuracy of your answer, heads or tails, is to ask yourself, 'Is this the Truth?' Obviously you want to know the correct answer to this question, and I find that when I ask it, it is easy to keep all extraneous thoughts from my mind, to keep me focused. So if you got a *yes* to your initial question, and a *no* to, 'Is this the Truth?', the answer to your original question is *no*. This gives your unconscious one more chance to speak Truth to you.

To recap, here is the dowsing process that I'm suggesting you use when you want to ask *yes* or *no* questions with a pendulum:

1. Frame the question in your mind. Think it through remembering that wherever the answers come from, your questions are taken quite literally. When you are ready, take out your pendulum.

2. This is what I want to do.

3. Can I?

4. May I?

5. Am I ready?

6. State the question.

7. I wonder what the answer's going to be? I wonder what the answer's going to be?

8. The answer.

9. Is this the Truth?

10. Return to step 6. (You should begin each dowse with steps 1–5 but you do not need to repeat these steps for every question.)

Using this process will maximize the possibility of you getting a useful 'correct' answer. And this is what a good dowser does. He or she spends a lot of time making sure that the right question is being asked before proceeding in a clear fashion to tune in and to check the results.

THE LEADING EDGE CONCEPT

Another way to use the pendulum has to do with the concept of the leading edge. This is a term for following the direction of the furthest swing of the pendulum away from you. Let's say that you are lost in the woods, and your main concern is to find your car. You ask your pendulum to assume your *search position* and frame your question. 'I want to know the direction of my automobile. Can I? May I? Am I ready?' Now once again go into the *search position*. If your *search position* is still, your pendulum will begin to swing back and forth. Watch the end of the swing that is initially away from you. This is called the leading edge.

In a period of fifteen or twenty swings of the pendulum, the leading edge can also take you around in a circle. If your *search position* is a back and forth swing, again watch the leading edge, the end of the swing that is initially away from you. (The 'forth' of back and forth.) Unless you are headed directly towards your car, the pendulum will swing back and forth, and the leading edge will begin to move in either a clockwise or counterclockwise direction. When the leading edge comes to a stop, and the pendulum just swings back and forth, it is pointing towards your vehicle. If, by some chance, your automobile is behind you, the leading edge will continue on around (over ninety degrees) until it is pointing in the direction of the car. (If your *search position* is still, and if the target is behind you, your pendulum will initially start oscillating, but then the leading edge will start to move around in one direction or the other until it is pointing towards the target.)

Try the leading edge concept with, 'Where's the nearest electrical outlet? Can I? May I? Am I ready? Where is the nearest electrical outlet to where I am presently sitting?' Watch that leading edge. When it stops and 'hangs on' to one direction, there is the socket!

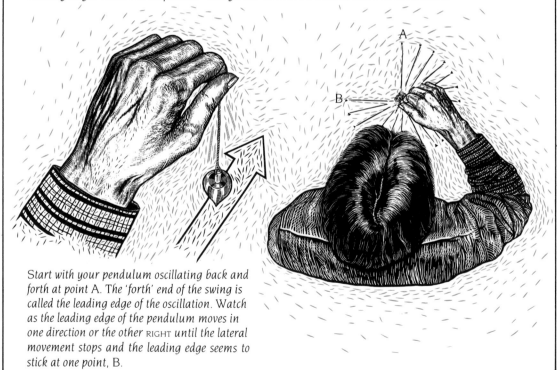

Start with your pendulum oscillating back and forth at point A. The 'forth' end of the swing is called the leading edge of the oscillation. Watch as the leading edge of the pendulum moves in one direction or the other RIGHT until the lateral movement stops and the leading edge seems to stick at one point, B.

TRIANGULATION

Dowsers use triangulation to identify the position of an object. Using the leading edge together with triangulation saves a lot of time.

Ask a friend to hide something, say a pencil, in the room. 'Where is the pencil?' (Notice that you don't need to go through 'Can I? May I? Am I ready?' because you've already done that for this dowsing session. I am assuming that you've carried on after the socket exercise.) Following the leading edge, find the direction, and draw an imaginary line from yourself in the direction that the leading edge of your pendulum pointed towards. So you gnow (intuitively know) *it is somewhere along that line, but where?*

Now go to some other place in the room, far away from where you were, and ask the same question, 'Now, in what direction is the pencil that my friend has hidden?' Draw that line, and where it intersects the first line, you should find the pencil. This is called triangulation, and it works even better as a double check when you shoot the target from three different locations. Tri (three) angulation (angles) saves a great deal of time, and is used by a number of excellent dowsers.

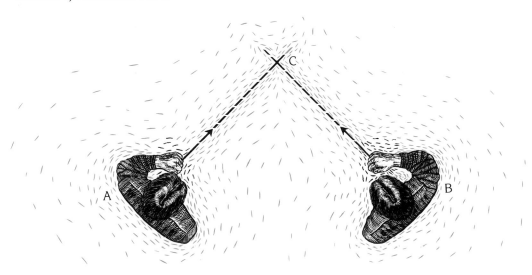

From point A, ask where the target is. Watch the leading edge and draw an imaginary line in that direction. Go to point B and repeat the same procedure. The target is found where the lines cross at Point C.

At some point, you may want to try this in a place with which you are not so familiar, like in a friend's home. Everyone has a broom and a dustpan, but where do they keep them? Some store them in the kitchen closet, others, in the cupboard by the front door. You can never be sure where it is. Try to pick a friend who won't be negative or suspicious about someone dowsing. Skepticism is not a useful environment in which to do early dowsing experiments — leave dealing with skeptics till later. Werner Heisenberg, a German physicist and philosopher, received the Nobel Prize for Physics in 1932 for his work in helping to establish quantum mechanics. Out of this work came the famous Heisenberg Uncertainty Principle, in which he showed that the observer is part of the process, and can affect the results of an experiment. 'Interactive' was the word he used to describe this relationship between the observer and the observed. Heisenberg has shown us that there's no such thing as a totally objective observer who is somehow completely detached from the observed. For this reason, choose the particular friend with some care. Look for someone who will be sympathetic to your dowsing request, not someone who would be skeptical or worse, antagonistic. As observer of your dowsing, your friend is part of the dowsing process you are involved in. Ask your pendulum.

Go in to your friend's living room and take some time to explain your intention. Talk about dowsing and the progress you are making. Pull out your pendulum and take a moment to center on what you're about to do. Remember, this isn't a party-game, you are doing this to expand your dowsing skills. Get your pendulum going in your search position. *'I want to find the broom and dustpan in this home. Can I? May I? Am I ready?'; all are* yes, *so, 'I want to* gnow *the direction of the nearest broom and dustpan in this home.' (There may be more than one set of these in the house.)*

As the pendulum starts going back and forth, watch the leading edge. When it stops, 'Is this the Truth?' If that's yes, go on to triangulate that line by walking somewhere else in the house and dowsing again. You may have to triangulate and follow the leading edge several times to get a sense of exactly where they are, but you may surprise yourself, and your friend, by ultimately walking right to them.

It's certainly exciting when exercises like this go well, and I trust that they are going that way for you, but if not, remember, we're still only at the beginning. Persevere, and keep doing the exercises.

For dowsers, the process of tuning in is a very important one. The ten steps that begin with, 'This is what I want to do,' and end with, 'Is this the Truth?' can be very helpful. The pendulum can clearly show direction using the leading edge concept and you must learn this skill to be able to operate the charts that will be covered in the next chapter.

Remember to run through the basic *search position, yes, no, maybe/wrong question* several times each day for at least a week. *Please* also do it again now before you start the next chapter.

CHAPTER 3

DOWSING CHARTS FOR FUN

By this time, I trust that the four basic pendulum movements of *search position*, *yes*, *no* and *maybe/wrong question* are working well. It really is important that you keep practicing these movements regularly, twice a day for at least a week. You should find by then that your growing confidence and skill will encourage you to keep dowsing.

The leading edge concept gives you powerful new ways of using the pendulum. In addition to finding in which direction something lies, the leading edge concept is also critical to working the charts, or fans, that are included in this book. The charts are called fans because they are sectioned like Oriental folded paper fans.

In this chapter, we will look at nineteen of these fans. They will run from a quite simple *yes*, *no* or *maybe* fan, and a straightforward Zero to One Hundred Chart, to a world map dowsing exercise that will have you locating known deposits of oil, and then fifteen charts that can help you to dowse and interpret problems and opportunities in your life using astrology as the vehicle for this process. The final fan, in conjunction with the Zero to One Hundred Chart, offers an unusual method of weather forecasting.

THE YES, NO, MAYBE CHART

The first chart uses the leading edge method demonstrated in the exercises that I trust you have been doing twice daily since you began this book. Look at chart number one.

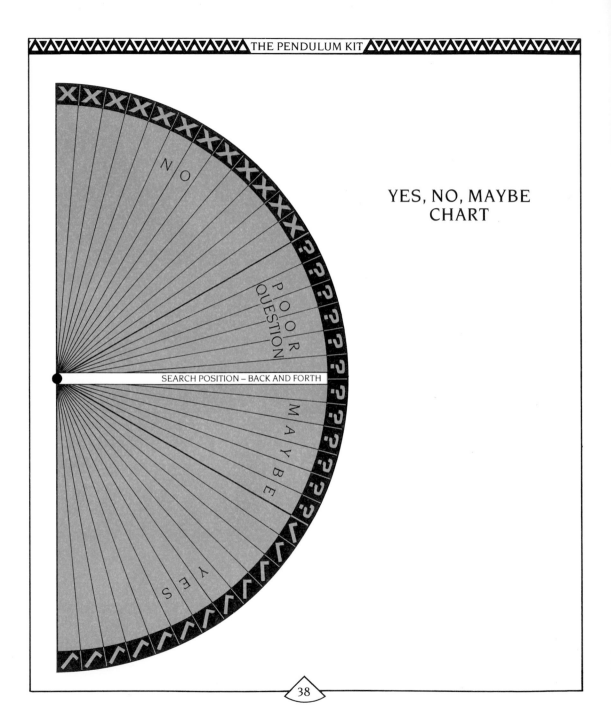

YES, NO, MAYBE
CHART

To work this chart, hold your pendulum over the point where all the three options merge in the bottom of the center of the chart or fan. This point is called the hinge. When you're ready, ask any question that can be answered by yes, no, or maybe. If you have established a stationary search position, your pendulum will start to oscillate after you ask the question, as if by itself, roughly in the direction of the answer. As your pendulum gains in strength and momentum, it will tune in on the exact answer, and seem to stick there.

If you have a back and forth search position, hold your thumb and forefinger directly

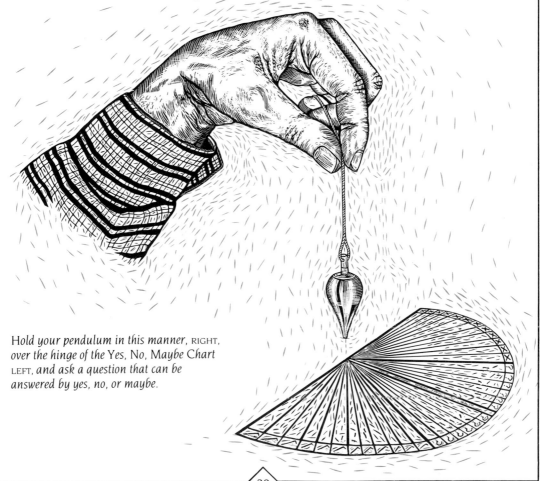

Hold your pendulum in this manner, RIGHT, over the hinge of the Yes, No, Maybe Chart LEFT, and ask a question that can be answered by yes, no, or maybe.

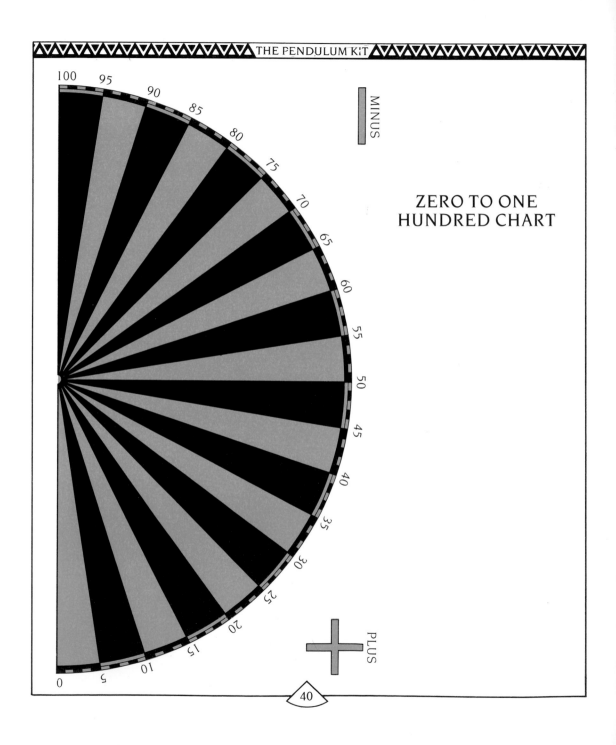

over the fan hinge, and start the pendulum oscillating somewhere in the middle of the chart. The leading edge of the pendulum, as if by itself, will start moving in one direction or the other. The answer comes at that point when the leading edge goes no further and the pendulum's oscillations stabilize in one direction.

During the time it takes from when you ask your question to when you get your answer, you should be saying to yourself, 'I wonder what the answer's going to be? I wonder what the answer's going to be?' so that your subjective desire for the answer to be, say, just to the left of where the pendulum seemed to start, doesn't sneak in to influence the direction. It's so easy to influence the pendulum.

Then ask, 'Is this the Truth?' - just to check again.

Hold your pendulum over the hinge, where the three options merge. Try the following question, 'Will this chart work for me?' Remember to do all the steps beginning with, 'This is what I want to do' and ending with, 'Is this the Truth?'. Watch the leading edge. I trust that all beginners would get a yes on this, but try the exercise anyway, for the experience.

You can now use this chart instead of the *yes, no, maybe* exercise I gave you earlier – or better yet, use them both. This chart can also be employed for the Twenty Questions game I mentioned earlier (page 20). The *yes/no* technique is very useful when you're using dowsing to determine a specific answer or to use as a final check when you have applied another dowsing technique. We'll discover lots of other uses for this chart as we go along.

THE ZERO TO ONE HUNDRED CHART

Another fan that's helpful is the Zero to One Hundred Chart. When you look at the chart, you will notice that the numbers run from right to left starting with zero in the right hand corner, climbing counterclockwise up the fan to 50 at the top, and down the sinistral side of the arc to 100 in the left-hand corner. The numbers run in the 'wrong' direction. This has been done on purpose. Jose Silva, a Texan who has developed the Silva Method, has been teaching people how to reach various levels of consciousness for many years now. His studies have shown that obtaining information by running your eyes from the left to the right (as you are when you read this sentence) tends to drive you into your left brain, or towards a more analytical mode. Conversely, the Silva Method teaches that consciously making your eyes run in the other direction, from right to left, tends to help you gain access to your right brain, or your more intuitive mode. The Zero to One Hundred Chart is thus designed to enable you to harness the power of your intuition just when you need to utilize this aspect of your being. You've asked all the objective, rational questions, and now you need to shift your awareness to your intuition to receive the answer.

The Zero to One Hundred Chart can be used in many different ways. For example, you can use it with books. Let's say that you find a book on Greek mythology. Take your pendulum out, and after the preparatory questions, you can ask the following, 'Assuming the worst book on Greek mythology is zero, and the best is 100, what number is this book?' If it's above 80, it's probably worth reading, if it's above 92 or 93, don't even put that book down, over 95, start reading it immediately!

Try it with this book, 'Assuming the best dowsing book for beginners is 100, and the worst is zero, where does Sig's book fit in for me?'

(I guess this means, assuming you tried the above exercise, that this book is worth continuing! Whew!)

Another use of this zero to one hundred scale has to do with personality. Establish that the biggest loser in the world is rated at zero, and your dream personality is one hundred. Start building up your own personality rating system with famous people, or your friends. It can be quite revealing.

There will be other uses of this zero to one hundred scale later in this book. We'll use it to check the temperature. We'll also look at other rating processes where the worst is zero, and the best is one hundred. It could prove, perhaps, to be one of the most useful of all the charts in this book.

THE WORLD MAP CHART

By now I trust that you have discovered that you don't need to be physically on top of something in order to dowse it. We have already done many dowsing exercises where there isn't any physical target and answers to *yes/no* questions are required. Where is the physical target with those kinds of questions? Furthermore, we have dowsed for a broom and dustpan in someone else's home without necessarily being in the same room as the cleaning tools. You don't *have* to be near a target in order to dowse its location.

When I was living in Glastonbury, in England, during the mid–1980s, my mother telephoned me from Vermont to tell me that her septic system was in need of repair. Nothing had been done on it since her mother first installed it during the 1940s, and now she didn't know where it was located. I had a picture of the ground plan of her house in my mind, and I dowsed that it was out from the back corner of the house to the east about 20 feet (6 m). A week later, she called to tell me that I had hit it 'spot on'. Most competent dowsers can do this. It is called remote dowsing, or map dowsing. Let's try it with the following chart.

Overleaf, there is a map of the world and you are going to locate all the known oil reserves with your pendulum. The exact locations of the oil fields are at the back of this book. The idea here is for you to test your fledgling dowsing skills, trying the technique called map dowsing. As you can see, the map of the world is divided up into a grid pattern, from 1–13 and A to Z.

Let's try using triangulation (see page 33). Hold your pendulum over one of the corners of the world map. After the initial questions, ask, 'Where's the nearest known oil reserve to this corner?' Note the imaginary line on which that deposit of oil exists. Go to either one of the adjacent corners, and ask, 'Where's that same deposit I just dowsed?' Draw this second line, and where the two lines converge, note the number and letter coordinates. Before you look at the answers, remember that all of the commonly accepted known oil reserves will be listed. Before you look then, tell your eyes that you only want to check that one grid coordinate. If you can successfully do that, you will be able to use this exercise more than once. If you don't think you can keep your eyes from straying to the other coordinates, you could perhaps ask a friend to check your answers for you — as you do when playing the childrens' game called Battleships.

Now check in the back of the book on page 126. You can quickly tell if you hit an oil

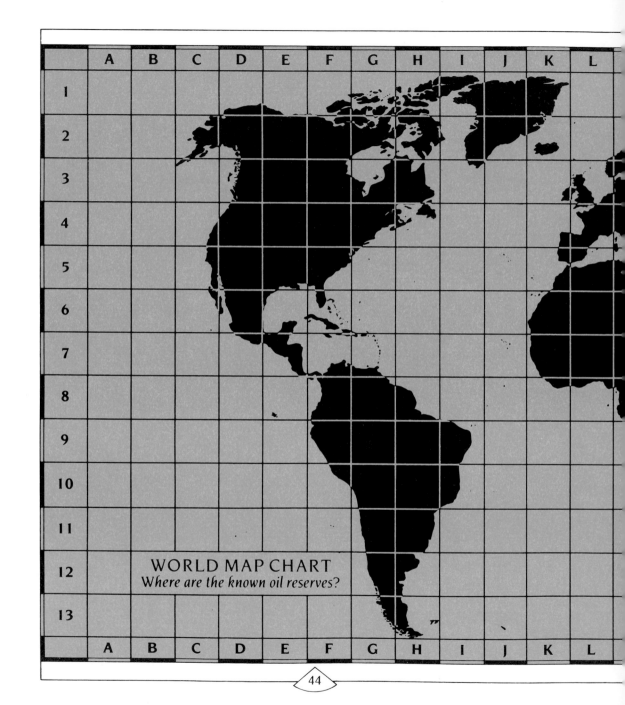

WORLD MAP CHART
Where are the known oil reserves?

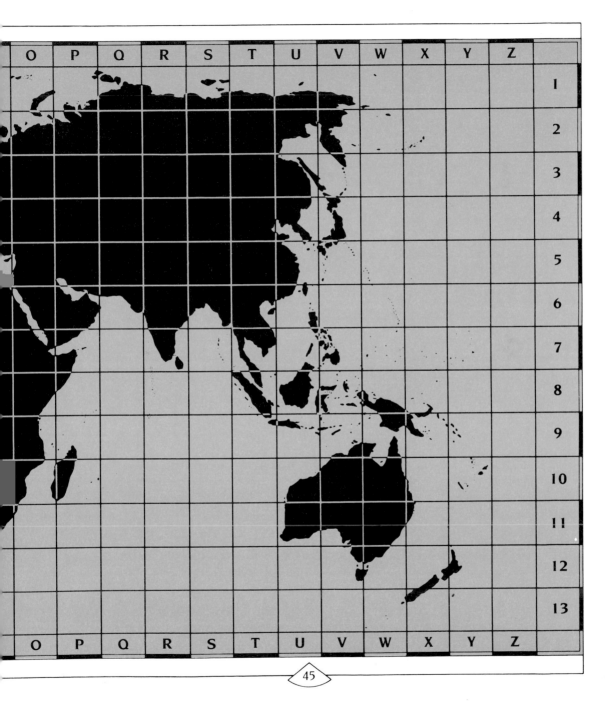

reserve. You didn't? If you drew a blank, try the same questions and method, but begin at a different corner, and triangulate again from an adjacent corner. When you have another coordinate, use your yes, no, maybe responses and ask, 'Are there underground reserves of oil here?'. If you get a yes, check your answer in the back of the book. If you get a no, check the coordinates of the squares adjacent to the one you triangulated.

Try to find other known deposits of oil on the map by phrasing your questions slightly differently. Try going down the edges of the map, and then triangulate. Notice that the vertical edge is numbered 1 to 13, and that the horizontal edge is lettered A to Z. Make the statement, 'I'm looking for a known oil deposit that I haven't dowsed yet.' Hold your pendulum away from the map and use the yes, no, maybe responses, as you run your finger down the left-hand vertical edge of the map. 'Is there an oil reserve in row number one? Number two? Number three?' Continue until you get a yes response. Now run your hand along the bottom edge of the world map. 'Is it in column A? Column B? Column C? Keep using this method until, once again, you get a positive response. One of the known oil reserves should lie at the intersection of the row and the column you have dowsed. Check on page 126 to see if you're right.

Remember, the scale of this world map is so large that pinpoint accuracy is not possible. It won't make you a J R Ewing! You would need a much smaller scale map of the specific area to do that. But they are available ...

THE ASTROLOGY CHARTS

To take us from the material world of underground oil deposits and book evaluations to the inner world of the self, here is a series of charts that deal with divining the inner you, through astrology. The most important thing that needs to be said right now is that you don't have to know anything at all about astrology to use these charts!

Do you know your Sun sign? Using the following list, you can easily find in which sign the Sun was found at the time of your birth.

Sun Signs and Birth Dates

Aries (♈) – Spring Equinox (circ. 21 March) to 20 April (page 50)
Taurus (♉) – 21 April to 21 May (page 51)

Gemini (♊) – 22 May to Summer Solstice (circ. 21 June) (page 52)
Cancer (♋) – Summer Solstice to 23 July (page 53)
Leo (♌) – 24 July to 23 August (page 54)
Virgo (♍) – 24 August to Autumn Equinox (circ. 23 September) (page 55)
Libra (♎) – Autumn Equinox to 23 October (page 56)
Scorpio (♏) – 24 October to 22 November (page 57)
Sagittarius (♐) – 23 November to Winter Solstice
   (circ. 21 December) (page 58)
Capricorn (♑) – Winter Solstice to 20 January (page 59)
Aquarius (♒) – 21 January to 19 February (page 60)
Pisces (♓) – 20 February to Spring Equinox (circ. 21 March) (page 61)

Over the years, the Equinoxes and Solstices vary by two or even three days, so the dates around those four times of the year vary as well.

I ask you to assume the position of a gnostic with the astrology charts, in that I'd like you first to be open to what they might have to say to you and *then* have you make up your own mind. Astrology isn't for everybody, but, in combination with dowsing (read: your intuition), astrology can give a uniquely individualized way of looking at yourself.

So, on that basis, please put aside what you might already know about astrology. If you've found that there's something to this study of the heavens that has been helpful in the past, fine, but try to start afresh. On the other hand, if you've found in the past that for you astrology is a load of bunkum, try to put that view aside as well – just for the time it takes to try dowsing over these charts.

The first twelve astrological charts that are the Sun Sign Charts begin on page 50. Please find yours.

Under the Sun sign itself, you will find a few words and phrases that describe typical characteristics of that sign, which part of the body the sign rules, and which element (Fire, Earth, Air, or Water) is associated with that sign.

For each of the Sun Sign Charts there are four areas of your life that you can dowse. They are Love, Happiness, Health, and Career. Here are some suggested questions you might like to begin by asking as you dowse your Sun Sign Chart:

1. How's my love life?
2. What makes me happy?
3. Which health issues do I need to be aware of?
4. What would be a good career (change) for me right now?

Beginning with your routine of, 'This is what I want to do. Can I? May I? Am I ready?', go to the chart with your Sun sign. At the corner marked 'Career' are five kinds of work that people with your Sun sign are generally good at. Hold your pendulum over the bottom right hand corner of the chart and ask, 'What would be a good career (change) for me right now?' Dowse the direction using the leading edge concept. You may already be involved with the career reading you have dowsed. On the other hand, you might be surprised by the result because it's something you've intuitively known you wanted to do but have never consciously thought about it!

Notice that there is also a section of the fan saying 'Go to zodiac' on it. If you get this reading, go to the Zodiac Wheel Chart (page 62). You will notice that this wheel contains the twelve signs of the zodiac on it. While many folks with your sign work well with the careers listed under your sign, you will apparently find yours in a different area.

Hold your pendulum over the center of the Zodiac Wheel Chart. Ask yourself, 'Which sign of the zodiac has the career (change) that would benefit me the most?' If your search position is back and forth, start it going on the line that separates Sagittarius and Capricorn at the top of the chart. Watch the leading edge until it stops and centers on a specific sign. If your search position is still, hold your pendulum over the center of the Zodiac Wheel Chart, and see towards which two opposing signs the pendulum oscillates. Point to one of the two signs, and using your yes, no, maybe responses ask, 'Is it this one?' If not, try the same question with the opposite sign. If you get a yes, 'Is this the Truth?'

Now go to the 'Careers' fan for that sign of the zodiac and dowse this instead of your own Sun sign.

When you do get an answer to the question, 'What would be a good career (change) for me right now?' ask your pendulum, 'Is this the Truth?' (If the answer is no, start over again.)

If yes, go on to the next category. For example, dowse the Health fan and ask, 'What health issues do I need to be aware of?' You may get an answer or you might be directed to go back to the Zodiac Wheel Chart. Move around the chart in this way.

Each category within one Sun Sign Chart reveals characteristic responses of people who have that specific sign. Some of them may not seem particularly pleasant, especially in the Health area, but pay attention to what your intuitive side is trying to tell you. You may not have that disease or difficulty right now, but you might have a tendency toward problems in that area. Keep an eye on it.

Also, some of the possibilities in the various categories have been put in the charts for their humor value. If your pendulum should go to one of them, there's sure to be a grain of truth for you to ponder.

If you find yourself in a quandary about a particular answer your pendulum gives you, you can work on it further by using the *yes, no, maybe* responses. Sometimes the answers that make the least sense are the most important. to understand. While it is always nice to hear something that confirms what you already know, I urge that you pay most attention to the answer(s) that don't seem to make immediate sense. They are important and should be kept in mind during subsequent readings. (They are 'food for the long haul'.)

The Sun Sign Charts can help you discover ways of dealing with specific situations. The following example will illustrate this.

Say you're having a problem with your love life. Say you are a Leo, and your partner is an Aquarius. Try dowsing the Love fan on each of these charts. For yourself in Leo you dowse the reading, 'Dynamic'. For your Aquarian partner you get 'Go to zodiac'. Go to the Zodiac Wheel Chart on page 62. It has all of the twelve signs of the zodiac. Hold your pendulum over the central hinge of the wheel and watch the leading edge (see page 31). Determine which of the twelve signs to go to (in this case, let's say it's Capricorn). Think of your partner and dowse the Capricorn Love fan. Say that the pendulum points to the reading 'Inhibited'. With your 'Dynamic' and your partner's 'Inhibited', perhaps you're coming on too strong and appearing to dominate your partner. Back off a little. Give your relationship — and your partner — some space.

ARIES
Assertively, Urgently, Rules the head
ELEMENT: FIRE

LOVE

HAPPINESS

Passionate

Starting new projects

Come on strong/low in stamina

Energetic

Taking chances

Drag racing/accelerating

Free style rock climbing

Love at first sight

A good debate

Go to zodiac (page 62)

Demonstrative

Go to zodiac (page 62)

Head injuries

Inventor

You are in great physical shape

Beginning a business

Accident prone

Fire-eater

Acne

Executive position

Tension/headaches

Pioneer/explorer

Go to zodiac (page 62)

Go to zodiac (page 62)

HEALTH

CAREERS

TAURUS
Possessively, Permanently, Rules the throat
ELEMENT: EARTH

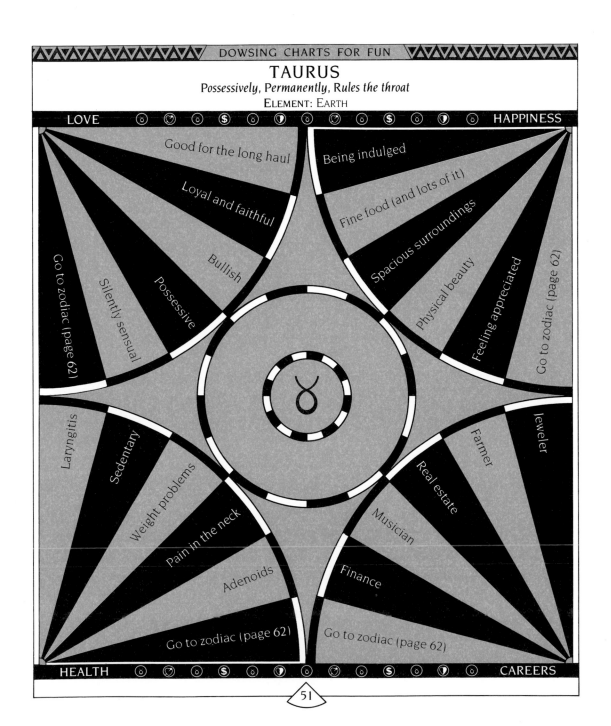

LOVE

HAPPINESS

Good for the long haul

Being indulged

Loyal and faithful

Fine food (and lots of it)

Spacious surroundings

Bullish

Physical beauty

Go to zodiac (page 62)

Silently sensual

Possessive

Feeling appreciated

Go to zodiac (page 62)

Laryngitis

Jeweler

Sedentary

Farmer

Weight problems

Real estate

Pain in the neck

Musician

Adenoids

Finance

Go to zodiac (page 62)

Go to zodiac (page 62)

HEALTH

CAREERS

GEMINI
Communicatively, Adaptability, Rules the lungs and hands
ELEMENT: AIR

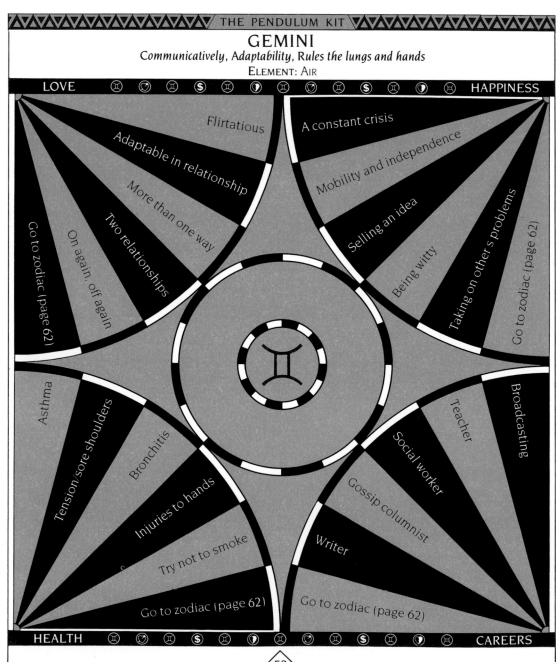

LOVE

HAPPINESS

Flirtatious

A constant crisis

Adaptable in relationship

Mobility and independence

More than one way

Selling an idea

Two relationships

Being witty

On again, off again

Taking on other's problems

Go to zodiac (page 62)

Go to zodiac (page 62)

Asthma

Broadcasting

Tension sore shoulders

Teacher

Bronchitis

Social worker

Injuries to hands

Gossip columnist

Try not to smoke

Writer

Go to zodiac (page 62)

Go to zodiac (page 62)

HEALTH

CAREERS

CANCER
Sensitively, Protectively, Rules the breasts and womb
ELEMENT: WATER

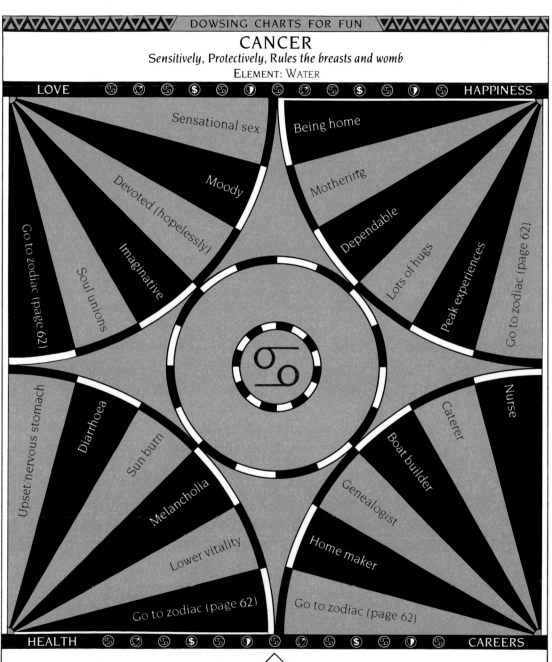

LOVE

HAPPINESS

Sensational sex

Being home

Moody

Mothering

Devoted (hopelessly)

Dependable

Imaginative

Lots of hugs

Peak experiences

Soul unions

Go to zodiac (page 62)

Go to zodiac (page 62)

Upset/nervous stomach

Diarrhoea

Sun burn

Melancholia

Lower vitality

Nurse

Caterer

Boat builder

Genealogist

Home maker

Go to zodiac (page 62)

Go to zodiac (page 62)

HEALTH

CAREERS

LEO
Creatively, Impressively, Rules the heart
ELEMENT: FIRE

LOVE — HAPPINESS

Generous

Being indulgent

Dynamic

Winning

The Lion's share

Unconventionality

Faithful

Gambling

Hedonistic

A full social calendar

Go to zodiac (page 62)

Go to zodiac (page 62)

Actor

Heart problems

Blood disorders

Sergeant

Try jogging

Politician

Spinal issues

Dancer

High fevers

Teacher

Go to zodiac (page 62)

Go to zodiac (page 62)

HEALTH — CAREERS

VIRGO

Critically, Analytically, Serving the whole, rules the stomach

ELEMENT: EARTH

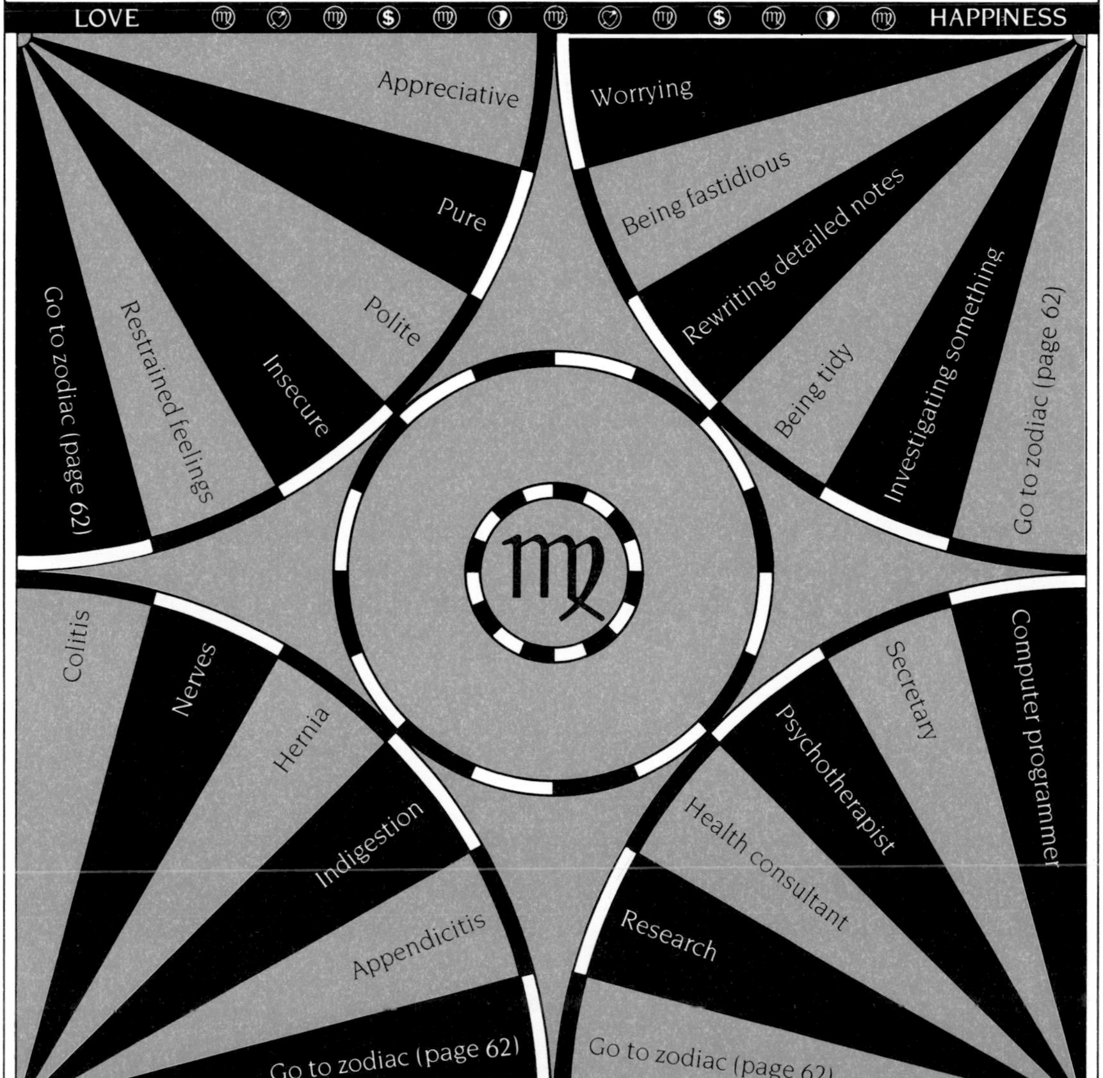

LOVE ♍ ☿ ♍ $ ♍ ☽ ♍ ☿ ♍ $ ♍ ☽ ♍ HAPPINESS

Appreciative

Worrying

Pure

Being fastidious

Polite

Rewriting detailed notes

Insecure

Being tidy

Go to zodiac (page 62)

Restrained feelings

Investigating something

Go to zodiac (page 62)

Colitis

Nerves

Secretary

Hernia

Computer programmer

Indigestion

Psychotherapist

Health consultant

Appendicitis

Research

Go to zodiac (page 62)

Go to zodiac (page 62)

HEALTH ♍ ☿ ♍ $ ♍ ☽ ♍ ☿ ♍ $ ♍ ☽ ♍ CAREERS

LIBRA
Harmoniously, Comfortable compromise, Rules the kidneys
ELEMENT: AIR

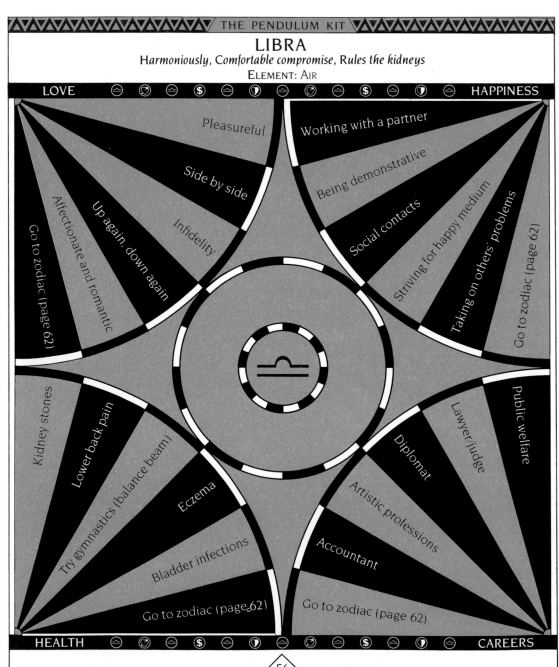

LOVE

HAPPINESS

Pleasureful

Working with a partner

Side by side

Being demonstrative

Infidelity

Social contacts

Striving for happy medium

Affectionate and romantic

Up again, down again

Taking on others' problems

Go to zodiac (page 62)

Go to zodiac (page 62)

Kidney stones

Lower back pain

Try gymnastics (balance beam)

Eczema

Bladder infections

Go to zodiac (page 62)

Public welfare

Lawyer/judge

Diplomat

Artistic professions

Accountant

Go to zodiac (page 62)

HEALTH

CAREERS

SCORPIO
Passionately, Intensively, Rules the genitals
ELEMENT: WATER

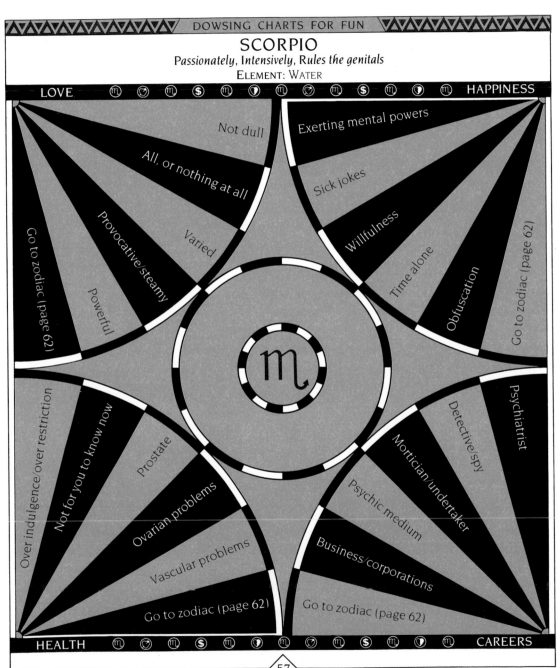

LOVE ♏ ♏ ♏ $ ♏ ☽ ♏ ♏ ♏ $ ♏ ☽ ♏ HAPPINESS

Not dull

Exerting mental powers

All, or nothing at all

Sick jokes

Provocative/steamy

Varied

Willfulness

Time alone

Go to zodiac (page 62)

Powerful

Obfuscation

Go to zodiac (page 62)

Psychiatrist

Over indulgence/over restriction

Not for you to know now

Prostate

Detective/spy

Ovarian problems

Mortician/undertaker

Vascular problems

Psychic medium

Business/corporations

Go to zodiac (page 62)

Go to zodiac (page 62)

HEALTH ♏ ♏ ♏ $ ♏ ☽ ♏ ♏ ♏ $ ♏ ☽ ♏ CAREERS

SAGITTARIUS
Expansively, Exploratively, Rules the pelvis and thighs
ELEMENT: FIRE

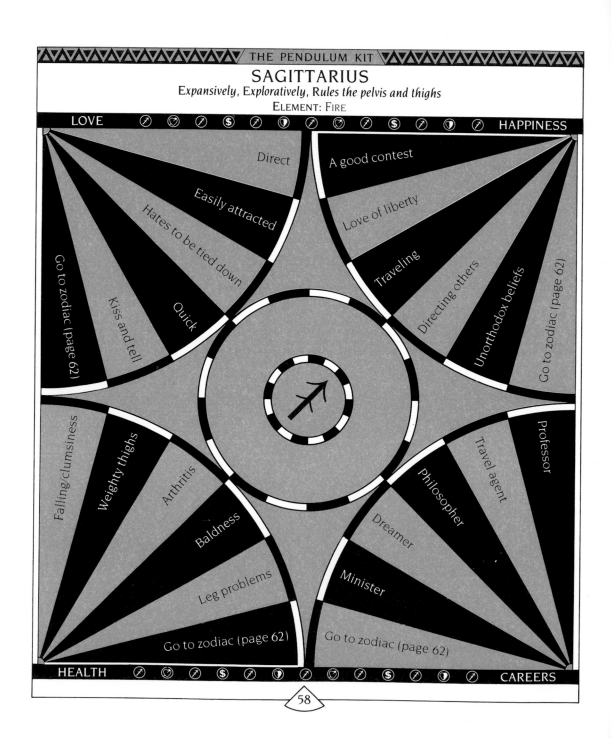

LOVE

HAPPINESS

Direct

A good contest

Easily attracted

Love of liberty

Hates to be tied down

Traveling

Go to zodiac (page 62)

Directing others

Unorthodox beliefs

Go to zodiac (page 62)

Kiss and tell

Quick

Falling/clumsiness

Weighty thighs

Arthritis

Professor

Travel agent

Philosopher

Baldness

Dreamer

Leg problems

Minister

Go to zodiac (page 62)

Go to zodiac (page 62)

HEALTH

CAREERS

CAPRICORN
Aspiringly, Prudently, Rules the knees
ELEMENT: EARTH

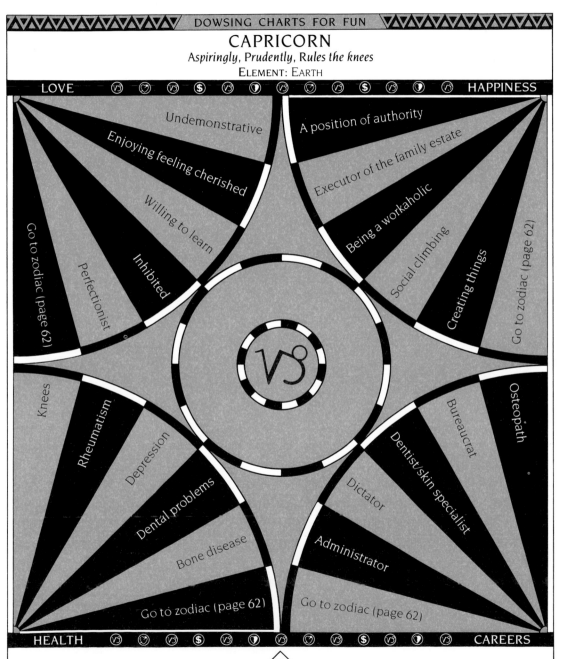

LOVE · HAPPINESS

Undemonstrative
Enjoying feeling cherished
Willing to learn
Inhibited
Perfectionist
Go to zodiac (page 62)

A position of authority
Executor of the family estate
Being a workaholic
Social climbing
Creating things
Go to zodiac (page 62)

Knees
Rheumatism
Depression
Dental problems
Bone disease
Go to zodiac (page 62)

Osteopath
Bureaucrat
Dentist skin specialist
Dictator
Administrator
Go to zodiac (page 62)

HEALTH · CAREERS

PISCES
Impressionably, Selflessly, Rules the feet
ELEMENT: WATER

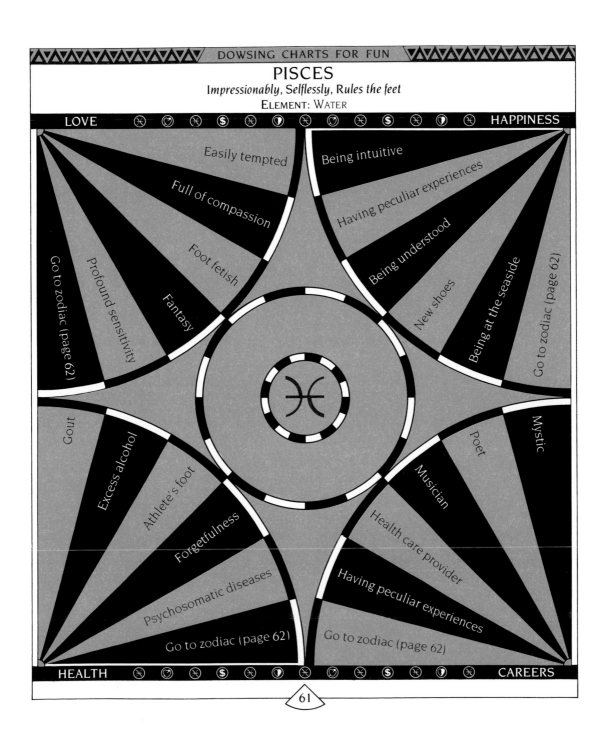

LOVE

HAPPINESS

Easily tempted

Being intuitive

Full of compassion

Having peculiar experiences

Foot fetish

Being understood

Profound sensitivity

New shoes

Fantasy

Being at the seaside

Go to zodiac (page 62)

Go to zodiac (page 62)

Gout

Mystic

Excess alcohol

Poet

Athlete's foot

Musician

Forgetfulness

Health care provider

Psychosomatic diseases

Having peculiar experiences

Go to zodiac (page 62)

Go to zodiac (page 62)

HEALTH

CAREERS

ZODIAC WHEEL CHART
How will the issue best be resolved?

THE ASTROLOGICAL HOUSES CHART

If you want to continue the search for yourself a bit further, you may want to work with the Astrological Houses Chart, (page 65). When you stop to consider, our lives are divided up into different areas: our feelings about ourselves; our relationships with our families, friends and peers; our jobs and social organizations, to mention a few.

Different divination systems divide our lives up into different numbers of slices, or areas. These divinatory 'pies' represent our totality, and the slices or divisions are the different scenes in which our totality can manifest itself. The Tarot cards divide up into seventy-eight slices, or cards. The I Ching is divided into sixty-four pieces called hexagrams; the Norse people broke it into twenty-one parts called runes. The yin/yang tennis ball symbol divides totality into only two slices.

This ancient Chinese symbol depicts the ultimate balance between the receptive yin, and the active yang forces found in the universe. It shows that it is impossible to have, say, a totally yang energy, since at its heart there is always yin.

In astrology, the astrological chart divides our lives into twelve areas. Each area corresponds to a particular sign of the zodiac (Aries, Taurus, Gemini etc.). Each sign of the zodiac has a natural correspondence with one of the twelve houses. There are lots of books that can help you understand the complex interrelationships of planetary and zodiacal archetypes (some are recommended in the 'Books To Read' section on page 120). The point of the Astrological Houses Chart is to increase your awareness of the energies that are available to you in each of the twelve zodiacal aspects of life, and how to use these energies.

The twelve houses are the various stages on which we play our lives – the personal, family, business and social areas of our life. The First House talks about the part of our totality that has to do with 'you-awareness', who you are and how you present yourself to the rest of the world. The Second House 'stage' has to do with that part of your life where you work with your personal resources; and so on, around the circle in a counterclockwise direction, through early education, your home, love life, health, and job to higher education, aspirations, status, and we-awareness, to the closing of the cycle when it is time to seek after a new self.

There are many ways that a chart like this can be used (just as there are other ways that you can use the Sun Sign Charts). You could try working with an issue that arose while you were dowsing the Sun Sign Charts. You can explore the issue further by using your *yes, no, maybe* responses together with the Astrological Houses Chart. The next exercise illustrates the technique. Let's say that you're feeling apprehensive about something, but you don't exactly know where your feeling is coming from.

Go to the Astrological Houses Chart. The First House should be to your left, between 8:00 and 9:00 on the face of a clock. Take out your pendulum and ask, 'I want to explore the reason that I'm feeling apprehensive. Can I? May I? Am I ready?' Assuming all yes, hold the pendulum directly over the center of the chart.

'Where is this apprehension primarily coming from? In what part of my life (slice of the pie) is this dark cloud to be mainly found?' If your search position is still, after a while, the pendulum will start moving back and forth with the middle of the arc just above the center of the chart, and the two extremes of the swing falling in two opposite houses. Point to one of the two houses and ask the question, 'Is this the House?' If the answer is yes, you gnow it is that house, if no, it's the opposite house. Don't forget, 'Is this the Truth?'

If you feel confident using the leading edge concept, you will probably find that it is a quicker way to obtain an answer. It doesn't require that second yes/no dowsing operation of, 'Is this the House?' (although it is always a good idea to check your answer.)

Let's say that you found your apprehensions were primarily centered in the Ninth House (Philosophy of life; Trips/spiritual journeys; Later/higher education; Religion/beliefs; Superconscious mind). 'This is where it's primarily coming from, but which specific area of

ASTROLOGICAL HOUSES CHART
Where will I resolve the issue?

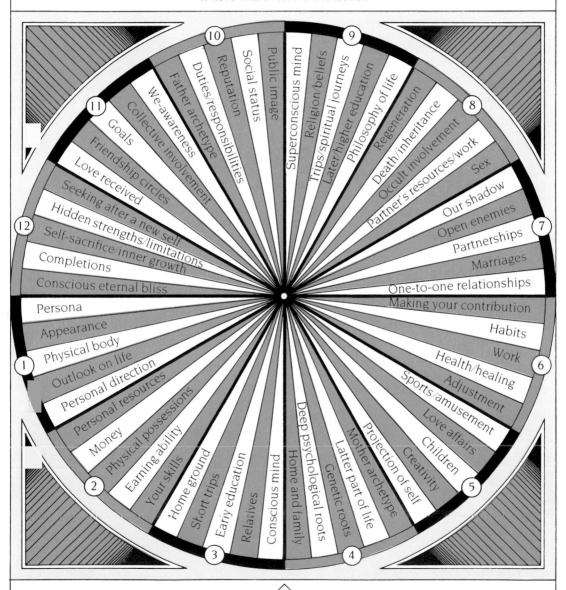

10 — Public image / Social status / Reputation / Duties/responsibilities / Father archetype / We-awareness / Collective involvement

11 — Goals / Friendship circles / Love received / Seeking after a new self / Hidden strengths/limitations

12 — Self-sacrifice/inner growth / Completions / Conscious eternal bliss

1 — Persona / Appearance / Physical body / Outlook on life / Personal direction / Personal resources

2 — Money / Physical possessions / Earning ability / Your skills / Home ground

3 — Short trips / Early education / Relatives / Conscious mind

4 — Home and family / Genetic roots / Latter part of life / Mother archetype / Deep psychological roots

5 — Projection of self / Creativity / Children / Love affairs / Sports/amusement

6 — Adjustment / Health/healing / Work / Habits / Making your contribution

7 — One-to-one relationships / Marriages / Partnerships / Open enemies / Our shadow

8 — Sex / Partner's resources/work / Occult involvement / Death/inheritance / Regeneration

9 — Philosophy of life / Later/higher education / Trips/spiritual journeys / Religion/beliefs / Superconscious mind

the Ninth House?' (At this point, I feel it is important to say, as a gnostic, that if you happen to be a student of astrology, and you use different words to remind yourself of what the Ninth House means for you, please, please use them. But let's assume for the purpose of this discussion that the words I have used feel appropriate.)

Using your own responses, or you could hold your pendulum over the Yes, No, Maybe Chart, ask, 'Is this apprehension found primarily in my philosophy of life?' No. 'Is it higher education later on in life?' Yes. 'Is it in any of the other areas in the Ninth House?' No. 'Is this the Truth?' Yes.

So you gnow that you have some apprehension around higher education. Have you been thinking about going for an academic degree or some adult education?

You don't relate to this piece of information? Hold your pendulum in the center of your own Sun Sign Chart. Put your pendulum in the search position and see whether it goes for Love, Happiness, Health, or Career. This will give you an idea of where you might benefit from some further education. For example, under Happiness, it may mean that the rock climbing you're doing for recreation is becoming too dangerous, and it's time to go to advanced climbing school; on the other hand, if it's under Career, perhaps it's really time to go back to school and update your job skills. The findings under the Love section can be just as revealing. Maybe you need practice, or to learn some advanced techniques. Tantra. There's always room for improvement. Likewise, the Health response might mean that you need to consider your nervous nature.

You can use the yes, no, maybe responses to ask further questions to clarify the situation. Remember to make your last question, 'Is this the Truth?'

You probably have a pretty good idea of what that apprehension you are feeling is about, but look back at the initial question — 'Where is this apprehension primarily coming from? In what part of my life is this dark cloud mainly found?' Using the same technique I have described, perhaps there are other areas or houses that could give you further information.

THE PLANETS CHART

There is another way to look at yourself from both a dowsing and an astrological point of view. It has to do with the different ways we approach life. The various roles we play are represented by the eleven known 'wandering stars' that astrologers work with. Of the first seven, five are the visible planets, Mercury, Venus, Mars, Jupiter, and Saturn. The other two visible wandering stars are termed 'luminaries' by astrologers. They are the Sun and the Moon. These seven inner planets represent the roles we play, the visible ways in which we manifest important aspects of ourselves: our essence; our feelings and thoughts; our love life; our assertive selves; how we expand our energies, and how we contract them.

Beyond Saturn are the planets that are invisible to the naked eye. As there are seven notes in our musical scale, which would represent the five visible planets plus the two luminaries (Sun and Moon), in some ways the four outer planets act as higher harmonics of the first seven; a higher octave. (Some astrologers feel that there are three more planets in our solar system yet to be discovered.)

The outer planets represent the less immediately visible ways in which we operate. Chiron (pronounced 'kyron') is the first of the 'invisible' planets. Discovered in the 1970s, Chiron's orbit takes it inside Saturn and almost to the orbit of Uranus, which is the next planet out. Regardless of whether astronomers agree that Chiron is a planet or not, like the Sun and the Moon, more and more astrologers are treating it like one. Beyond Uranus, which was discovered in 1781, are the last two presently known planets, Neptune, discovered in 1846, and Pluto, discovered in 1930. These four outer planets have to do with less tangible things like bringing us to resolution, or breaking us off from the past; the coming or rising of new awarenesses; altered states; transformation and renewal.

In the Planets Chart (page 69), you will find descriptions of various ways in which change can be brought about, perhaps through reflection, through the mind, through love, or through action. This chart answers questions like, 'How can I best deal with my father?' or, 'What will that change be like?' or, 'What role should I take to deal with this issue in the best way for all concerned?'

Since no one experiences a planet in its full power at any given time, it is usually best to dowse this chart two or three times to find not only the main role you are playing, but also to see if there are any subsidiary possibilities.

Perhaps an example would be helpful here. Let's say that you are having problems with your father and you dowse the Planets Chart to find out more, and you get Mercury which represents mind, oscillation, messages, the messenger, and communication. The mental back and forth of messages has to do with communication. Perhaps that is where the problem lies with your father – you're not communicating well with him.

So you dowse the Planets Chart again to see what other influences there might be in this communication issue you have with your father, and you get Saturn. Saturn has to do with limitations, restrictions, and rules. Are you feeling restricted by the present role you play with your father? Perhaps you're allowing him to trigger your unconscious, your feelings about the relationship you had with him when you were a kid, and that is still affecting you today, especially in your communications with him. Use the *yes, no, maybe* responses to check this out. Be aware perhaps, of those past resentments and fears, and don't let others push the button in you that gets those 'tapes' playing again, and again, and again.

Think about some issue you are working with in your life right now. The Planets Chart is a way to explore the various roles you can play in bringing about change. The wanderers in the sky represent various energies you can use to bring about resolution. Clearly state the issue. Honestly seek resolution. Hold your pendulum over the hinge of the Planets Chart, and ask something like, 'What must I do to bring about resolution to this issue? What kind of energy can I best use?' Likewise, 'Which of these planet/energies must I watch out for as they could work against resolution?' See what your pendulum has to say.

The planets represent the various archetypal roles or parts we can play in the various stages that the twelve houses set up for us. The houses speak of the stage on which the play of life will unfold, where it is going on. The signs of the zodiac speak to the theme, and tell us how things may potentially come about. By working back and forth on these different astrology charts, you can find out a great deal about yourself and others, if you should choose to use them that way.

Let's say that you are working on a problem with your friend. What can you do to bring about resolution, what role can you best play? State the problem, and hold your pendulum over the hinge of the Planet Chart and say, 'Which planet best addresses a problem like this?' When you get an answer, go on to

PLANETS CHART
What role should I take to resolve the issue?

THE SUN
Our center, our true self, conscious, individuality, the active.

THE MOON
Reflective, instinctual, the receptive, the unconscious, past/conditioning, am I safe?

MERCURY
Roman messenger of the gods. Mind oscillation, messages, messenger, communication.

VENUS
Roman goddess of love. Loving and or being loved, heart energy, attraction, artistic.

MARS
Roman god of war. Assertiveness, drive, making things work out, activity.

JUPITER
King of the roman gods. Understanding, power, investment, expansion, joviality.

SATURN
Roman god of harvest, Father time. Restrictions, self-limitations, responsibilities, the rules, commitment.

CHIRON
Greek Centaur, Healer, priest and wise teacher. Dances between the visible and the invisible, paradox and resolution, answers.

URANUS
Greek sky god, Father of the titans. New uncharted country, separation, awakens the intuition, radical changes.

NEPTUNE
Roman king of the sea. Expansion of consciousness, confusion, altruism, mystical.

PLUTO
Roman king of the underworld. Confrontation, transformation, sudden illumination/change.

the Astrological Houses Chart, and ask, 'Where is the stage, in which part of my life, in which house, will this be enacted?' Go to the Zodiac Wheel Chart. Hold your pendulum in the center, and ask, 'How will I know this resolution? What sign will I see?' Your leading edge will lock on to one of the twelve signs. Go to that sign with its four fans for Love, Happiness, Health, and Career. On the chart of that sign are the sign's name, the astrological symbol of that zodiacal sign, and several words and phrases that describe that sign. These words deal with the question, 'How?' You can pinpoint what you're looking for by dowsing any of the four fans for that sign as well.

You can use these charts for a quick read, a quick divination, any time you're faced with uncertainty. When you have a stated problem/opportunity, the planets answer the question, 'What?' The houses answer the question, 'Where?' And the sign of the zodiac answers the question, 'How?' (The four fan charts enable you to be even more specific.)

WEATHER DOWSING

I've saved the issue of dowsing the weather until last because in some ways, it is the most difficult for some dowsers – dowsing the future and the trend. Recently, I've been working with a colleague, Dr Eleanor Ott, on dowsing the weather. We've been interested in two specific questions:

1. *What will the temperature be when I look at my outdoor thermometer for the first time tomorrow morning?*

2. *What will I see in the sky when I look at it for the first time tomorrow morning?*

The Zero to One Hundred Chart can be of immediate use to determine the temperature. After tuning in, hold your pendulum over the hinge of the chart and ask the first question. Follow the leading edge until it sticks at a certain reading. It can tell you the temperature to the nearest degree.

If you live in a climate where the temperature goes below zero degrees (Fahrenheit or Centigrade, it doesn't make any difference) you will have to be able to tell if your degree reading is above or below zero. If you live in a tropical climate, this may seem like an irrelevant problem, but where I live in Vermont, the temperature varies from over 100 degrees Fahrenheit (38°C) in the summer to 45 degrees *below* zero (−42°C) on a deep January winter night.

Interestingly enough, when Eleanor and I worked with these questions, it was in November, December, and January, times of the year when my outdoor Fahrenheit thermometer dances above and below zero. Actually, within one six day period, the morning readings began at 15 degrees Fahrenheit above zero (−9°C), went down to 20 below zero (−28°C), and back up to 40 degrees above zero (4°C) all within one week! The problem here is one's preconception of what the weather's going to be. 'It was 20 below last night, it ought to be another cold one tonight.' And it was 40 degrees Fahrenheit above the next morning, a difference of 60 degrees Fahrenheit! If you live in a climate where the temperature varies relatively little, your task is much easier!

Notice that, the Zero to One Hundred Chart (page 40) has a plus (+ = yes) and minus (− = no) on it. If you live in a climate where at a particular time of year the temperature bobs above and below zero, you can use the chart to check for this as well.

You can use the Yes, No, Maybe Chart (yes = +, no = −), or your yes, no, maybe responses, or you can hold your pendulum over the plus sign on the Zero to One Hundred Chart and ask, 'Will the reading on my outdoor thermometer tomorrow morning be above zero degrees?'

If the answer is no, hold it over the minus sign on the same chart, and ask, 'Will it be below zero tomorrow morning?' If the answer is yes, you know that you've double checked that the reading will be below zero. 'Is this the Truth?'

Then you can put your pendulum on the hinge and ask, 'What will the temperature be when I look at my outdoor thermometer for the first time tomorrow morning?'

Watch the leading edge, and it will stick on one particular number. 'Is this the Truth?'

Eleanor and I have developed a seven point chart of possible answers to the question, 'What will I see the first time I look at the sky tomorrow morning?' The possibilities are snow, rain, fog, totally cloudy, enough blue to make a shirt, mostly blue, totally blue/cloudless.

SKY TOMORROW MORNING CHART
What will I *see the first time* I *look at the sky tomorrow morning?*

Hold your pendulum over the hinge of the Sky Tomorrow Morning Chart, and ask the following question, 'What will I see the first time I look at the sky tomorrow morning?' Follow the leading edge to the answer.

The best time to begin your temperature and sky dowsing is on the previous night, just before you get into bed. Keep track of your dowsing results, together with the morning temperatures and sky conditions, on a notepad. If you don't happen to have an outdoor thermometer, and you use the radio to give you morning temperature readings, then rephrase your question.

One word of warning:there's potentially a very high frustration factor built in to this method of weather dowsing. If it doesn't seem to work, spend some time analyzing your dowsing process. Have you cut corners? Was it the right question? Even if you don't become proficient at dowsing the weather, you can learn a great deal about how your dowsing skills are progressing.

When Eleanor and I were beginning, we used what astrologers call orbs in order to increase our success rate. Say, for instance, that any temperature within five degrees is considered close enough to be successful. Maybe a three degree orb is better. But then, if the idea is to hit the exact temperatures, why use orbs at all? It's up to you.

The charts covered in this chapter can be used in many different ways. If you can dowse a map of the world for underground reserves of oil, you can dowse any map or photograph for almost anything. Your use of the astrology charts is limited only by your own imagination. The weather chart might prove to be a fun experiment or a frustrating, learning experience.

One final note on dowsing and astrology brings me to Mercury in particular. One of the keywords used by many astrologers to describe Mercury, the messenger of the gods, is oscillation, or as my friend, astrologer Palden Jenkins, says, 'much to-ing and fro-ing.'

This is exactly what the pendulum does. It oscillates. It goes, like Mercury, back and forth and to and fro. The pendulum is a messenger, a tool of Mercury that can take us from the rational to the intuitive, from the known to the intuitively known, or *gnown*. Find meaningful ways to use your pendulum as a messenger in your daily routine, and you will have a friend for life.

CHAPTER 4

DOWSING APPLICATIONS

T oo many dowsers, who have some initial success with their pendulums, find that after a while, they have less and less use for dowsing, and then they stop altogether. The trick is to do just the opposite and see if you can find more and more ways to use dowsing. Exercise that intuition of yours! There are all kinds of ways to successfully dowse in your home. For example, the pendulum can come in handy when you lose something. It doesn't always work because you must be careful to ask the right questions, but sometimes the results can be astonishing. You may remember my experience with an engagement ring lost on the lawn.

We'll start by developing the set of pendulum signals that indicate when you are approaching the target, when you're directly over it, and some exercises to practice. We'll explore some of the things people look for with their pendulums, and give more tips on map dowsing. Then we'll examine the potential for dowsing and nutrition and discovering your own food allergies. The flower remedies that work directly with your emotions might be new to you, but dowsing with them may open up new possibilities. You might find that they work well with the Astrology Charts you used in chapter 3.

What do you do when you've lost something and let's say you're sure it's in your home? Take out your pendulum, of course! Use the leading edge technique to show you the direction of the lost object, and as you move in that direction towards it, the pendulum demonstrates when you are getting close to the target, and then, that you are over the target and even whether

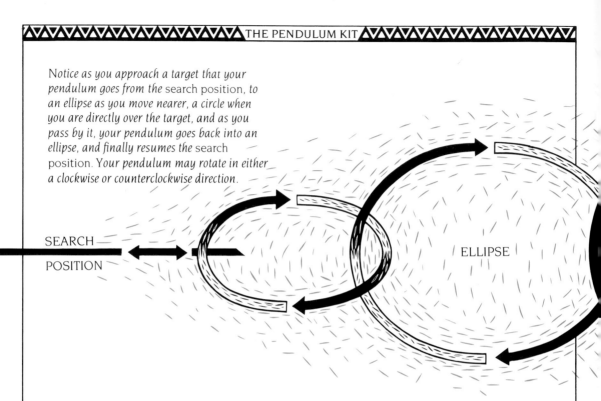

Notice as you approach a target that your pendulum goes from the search position, to an ellipse as you move nearer, a circle when you are directly over the target, and as you pass by it, your pendulum goes back into an ellipse, and finally resumes the search position. Your pendulum may rotate in either a clockwise or counterclockwise direction.

SEARCH POSITION

ELLIPSE

you have actually gone beyond the lost object. Most dowsers find that seeking direction *and* position is a very useful skill to develop and perfect. Here is an exercise for you to practice.

Put a coin on a table in front of you. Take a moment to tune in. Using the leading edge technique, tell the pendulum to show you the direction of the coin. (I know that you can see the coin, but for the purpose of this exercise, pretend that you can't.)

Starting in whichever search position you use, move your hand along the imaginary line that the leading edge and the oscillation of the pendulum are showing you. As you approach the coin target, your pendulum will begin to make an ellipse shape. Your thumb and forefinger are moving along the major axis of the ellipse, as your hand moves towards the target. When you get still closer, the ellipse becomes more and more circular, until, when your pendulum is directly over the target, the pendulum is swinging in a perfect circle. As your hand goes beyond the coin, the path of the pendulum will become elliptical again, and

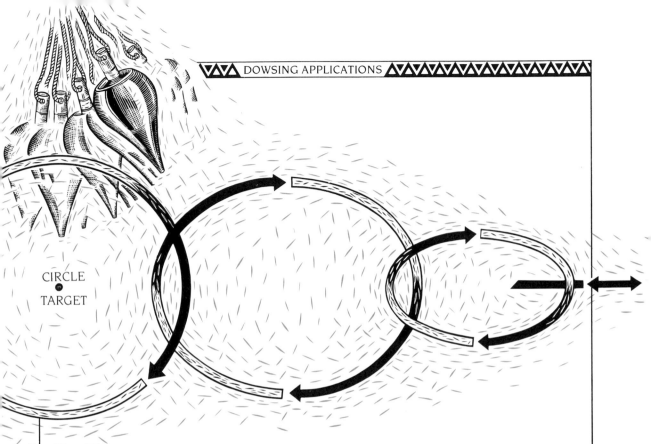

CIRCLE
• TARGET

the further away you move from the target, the more flattened out that ellipse becomes until your pendulum is just going in the back and forth or stationary search position.

Now place a book as a target on the floor on the other side of the room. Try the same exercise you carried out with the coin, but standing up. The major difference you will encounter is that the distance from the target when your pendulum first goes into an ellipse will become much greater. On the table, this distance was measured in inches; when you use your whole body, that distance becomes 3 to 5 feet (1–1½ m). Please try this exercise now. You may find that it feels strange to be standing but as your pendulum swings don't hesitate because you will find that the reaction is lost completely. Try to be aware of what you are doing, without concentrating so hard that you force the response.

Notice that, so far, I've said nothing about which way the pendulum rotates, either clockwise or counterclockwise. For the above exercises, it doesn't make a bit of difference. It can go either way, and be equally effective.

You now have the skills to find anything you can think of. A carpenter I know uses his plumb bob to dowse the studs in the interior walls of houses. Maybe you can find that lost ring or other piece of jewelry now. When something is broken or has simply ceased working, but you can't find out why, you can use your pendulum to find out which part is not working. A Canadian dowser I was told about used his dowsing skills to find specific problems in the engines of automobiles. Others have used it to find out which part of a main frame computer wasn't working!

Don't forget to combine your searching skills with map dowsing. It saves so much time if you've got a lot of ground to cover. All you need is a drawing of the place where you want to dowse. It can be a topographical map, a photograph, or a simple free-hand drawing of the place you're searching. Use either triangulation or the column and row techniques you learned using the World Map Chart (page 44).

Home map dowsing is also very efficient. If you think you lost something in your home, draw a floor plan of the house as if you were looking down through the roof. After the usual introductory questions, ask your pendulum, 'Is what I'm looking for in this house?' If it is, dowse the drawing exactly as you did for the World Map. Then go to that part of the house, and use triangulation to find the lost item.

A while ago, I went to the Basilica of Saint Anne de Beaupre, in Quebec, Canada. It is the most visited holy well and healing shrine in North America. As a student of the earth energies (the life systems of Earth), I *gnew* (intuitively knew) that there are always power centers at truly holy places like Saint Anne de Beaupre. In my mind, I studied the cruciform (cross-shaped) floor plan that is used so frequently in Catholic cathedral architecture. Normally the major earth energy center is found under the high altar at the far end of the choir pews, but in this case, my inner eye was drawn to the end of the left hand arm of the transept. (In layman's terms, the transept in a cathedral or basilica is architecturally the arms of a Christian cross.)

When I got to Saint Anne's, several hours later, I walked down the nave towards the high altar, and came to the transept. I looked to my left, and there, at the end of the transept, was the object of the pilgrimage of so many in need of healing. In addition to a wrist bone, said to have belonged to Saint Anne, the mother of Mary, there was a large circular column where supplicants knelt to pray. Hanging on that column was the mute evidence of Saint Anne's healing powers; glasses, canes, crutches, leg braces, and other paraphernalia no longer needed by the healed pilgrims. Indeed, the major power center for this basilica is in the left (northwest) arm of the transept. My map dowsing/intuition had been right on target.

DOWSING FOOD AND ALLERGIES

The pendulum can be of great use if you are on a diet of any kind. Many people today are on macro-biotic, candida (yeast), sugar-free, sodium-free, low cholesterol, low calorie, organic, or other diets. 'Is this food appropriate for me to eat?' is a typical question for the pendulum.

As a dowser, you will go through various rites of passage as you grow in your skills. For many, the 'Ah ha!' the first time a dowsing tool 'works by itself' (or at least truly feels that way) is just such a rite. Another occurs when you want to dowse in public for the first time.

When I first went on field trips with the New England Antiquities Research Association (NEARA), a group that is interested in enigmatic prehistoric archaeological sites in the northeastern United States, I didn't feel that I could just openly bring out my dowsing tools to look at the earth energies at the sites we were visiting. Most of the NEARA members were archaeologically inclined, and I feared dowsing might be anathema to them. I remember hiding behind a rock so I could ask my pendulum questions about the earth energies that were there. Finally, so many people came up to me and asked me what I was doing that I listened to the voice inside that said, 'Go for it!', and just pulled out my aura meter (an expensive dowsing tool that is very good at showing the edges of energy fields) and dowsed. The sky didn't fall in. Their reaction was an interested one! It never bothered me after that. I've even done some restrained dowsing in Gothic Cathedrals.

Betts Albright, a friend who ran the Annual Convention of the American Society of Dowsers for many years, unabashedly takes her pendulum to the grocery store to check out the freshness and ripeness of fruit and vegetables.

Going public is one phase most dowsers experience at some point in their careers. And here's where special diets come in. A friend of mine has hypoglycemia, and she told me that when she went to college, her parents had paid the school kitchen extra money to prepare food without sugar for her. Apparently the kitchen staff thought this request was ridiculous, and just gave her the same sugar-laden food that they gave everyone else. By the end of one semester, her metabolism was so out of balance that she thought she was having a nervous breakdown.

If she had dowsed her food, she would have *gnown* (intuitively known) that it wasn't good for her. As it was, she dropped out of school, and when she took responsibility for her own food preparation, all the hypoglycemic symptoms disappeared.

The Zero to One Hundred Chart can be helpful here as well. 'If the best food for me is one hundred and the worst junk food is zero, how do these french fries rate?' (But then, maybe you really don't need a pendulum for the answer to that question!)

Dowsing can also help in working with allergies, not only in identifying them, but in ascertaining if any foods you're allergic to are in what you are about to eat. If you are having some kind of allergic reaction, and you can't seem to discover what's causing it, ask your intuition. 'Is it something I'm eating? Is it something I'm breathing? Am I coming in contact with a substance when I go outside? Is it only one thing?' Through *yes* and *no* questions, you can narrow it down quite quickly. The Zero to One Hundred Chart can quickly show you how much any given substance can affect you.

A friend of mine in England, Freddie Fredericks, has long lists of foods that can cause allergic reactions, ranging from specific dairy products, through meats and vegetables, to exotic fruits. When she does a reading for someone else, she goes down the list with her pendulum in the search position. When she approaches a food that might cause an allergic reaction in that person, her pendulum lets her know that it's coming, and when she's directly over it, it tells her, 'This is the one.' You already have a system of doing this – as you go down the list, when you are approaching a food (target) to which you could be allergic, your pendulum will go into an ellipse, and then a circle when your hand is directly over the offending food.

Freddie also has lists of various chemicals that are used as additives in food. Dowsing can give you an indication of food additives to avoid. On the positive side, Freddie has a list of beneficial food supplements, the vitamins and minerals necessary for your well being. Let your intuition be your guide in combination with your rational mind. You know, for instance, that certain vitamins, like A and D, are not good to take in large doses.

You can make lists of foods and dowse them yourself, or you can create fans with different foods in each compartment. The questions you use are up to you. Just be sure that you have a specific question in mind.

Please don't feel limited by the charts that have been included with this book. You can make charts for anything you can think of that involves various choices. You could even dowse a destination for your next holiday!

THE FLOWER REMEDIES

While the pendulum can be of aid on the physical level in terms of which foods to eat, or what you may be allergic to, it can also be of inestimable value when working on the emotional level. One of the ways to work with the more incomprehensible emotions like anger, fear or grief is with flower remedies. The essences of certain flowers have been found to be actively helpful when working with emotional issues.

Let me give you an example. Let's say that you want to start recording your dreams, but you're having trouble remembering them. One of the flowers that has been found effective in this case is *Forget Me Not*, sometimes found in great profusion in a flower garden. It is almost a weed, with little light-blue flowers. If picked at noon and put with a small amount of good clean water in a crystal glass in the Sun for several hours, the essence of the blossoms is absorbed through the action of the sunlight.

The water is mixed 50–50 with a preservative such as brandy, or cognac. Most dosages then call for a few drops of this mixture to be taken with a glass of water. Alternatively, you could draw out some liquid through a small tube with a dropper, and take several drops on your tongue (you can dowse specifically how many) before going to sleep with the intent that you do not forget your dreams.

While it's always best to make these remedies yourself, there are several sets of commercially created flower essences on the market. One well known brand is made in England, and another is made in California, in the United States. Their names and how to obtain further information about them are in the back of this book (page 122). Needless to say, if you find that you have a serious medical problem, these remedies should be taken in conjunction with the advice of a trained health care provider or doctor.

The English Bach Flower Remedies offer essences that cover the entire range of emotions, from fear and uncertainty, through lack of interest in the present, loneliness, and over-sensitivity, to feelings of despondency and despair and excessive concern for the welfare of others. There are thirty-nine of these remedies including a special one called Rescue Remedy that is a compilation of five of the others, and is especially good for any kind of blow (physical or emotional), for shock, jet lag, or any severe upset. The Bach people publish a wonderful chart for dowsing these remedies called 'The Bach Flower Remedies: Natural Healing', that is available from them at any of their addresses on page 122. However, you don't necessarily need a commercially made chart; you can make one yourself with the next exercise.

Let's say that you happen to have some of the flower essence remedies, and that you have worked with the astrology charts that were introduced in Chapter Three. You may have become conscious of some unresolved feelings, brought to the surface when you dowsed the charts. Try to summarize those feelings into a keyword or two.

Now write down the names of the flower remedies you have available, or use a list provided by a local supplier, and dowse over them with your pendulum. After tuning in, say, 'When my hand is directly over the remedy that would be most useful to me now, show me yes.'

When you receive this positive response, ask, 'Is this the best one?' If yes, read about the therapeutic qualities of that remedy. If you can relate to it easily, that is great. If you can't, that is even better! In my experience, there are many times when your intuition can let you know about feelings of which you may not even be consciously aware. Pay close attention to *the dowsing results to which you feel you can't relate. Sometimes they are telling you something really important. This is especially true if you have a strong negative reaction when you discover the use of a flower remedy. (Always remember to ask, 'Is this the Truth?')*

Now use the Zero to One Hundred Chart to find out for how many days you need to take the drops. If your pendulum goes to zero, it means you need to take them for less than one day. Whenever you think of it (i.e. whenever your intuition reminds you), take a drop or two (dowse how much), as you think about the qualities of the remedy.

You might want to try the wholistic approach and mix this intuitively chosen remedy half-and-half with one that you have chosen rationally. Think again about the unresolved feelings that resulted from your work with the astrological charts, and then read through a list of flower remedies. Find the one that you think would best deal or resonate with your feelings. This rationally chosen remedy can often complement and enhance the one you intuitively chose using your pendulum. You should find that the astrology charts and the flower remedies can work together to produce powerful tools for personal transformation.

Forget Me Not is very useful in remembering a person's name, an important appointment, or, as mentioned above, remembering your dreams. More and more people are beginning to record their dreams in one way or another, working by themselves or with others to try and come to some understanding as to what they might mean. As dream interpretation is ultimately the responsibility of the dreamer, there is no correct way to interpret dreams.

However you use your pendulum, dowsing can help you with intuitive interpretation. If you are considering the theory that a certain object or symbol in a dream of yours represents something else, check it with your pendulum. You've been working with a particular character in one of your dreams; have you examined this character carefully enough? Ask your pendulum. At every step on the way to interpretation, decisions have to be made, and dowsing can enhance your intuitive process in those decisions.

WATER DOWSING

While many dowsers today, including myself, are interested in all kinds of esoteric dowsing like using the pendulum for healing, for looking at auras, and for dowsing earth energies at sacred places (see page 78), it is very clear to me that, by far the most critical dowsing skill on this planet in the next twenty-five years will be our ability to find reliable sources of good potable (drinkable) water.

To start with, pollution is affecting the drinking water reserves on the surface of the earth. Dowsers suggest that there is a different source of water that comes as the result of chemical reactions, from the depths of the earth. This water is called juvenile or primary, water and it is different from that drawn from the water table. Juvenile water hasn't been recycled through the familiar cycle of evaporation to clouds and then rain. In a sense it's brand new water. It's clean and never been used. It's usually quite potable. Juvenile water is what most water dowsers are looking for when they're seeking the place to drill a well.

But if you've never seen this juvenile water, or never felt its pull, how can you dowse for it? Nature has given us many different signs in both the vegetable and animal kingdoms of an affinity between veins of this special underground water and certain plants and animals. If you can find these signs, you can easily dowse over them to find juvenile water. The signs on the surface of the earth will give confirmation of your dowsing signals. Maybe you'll never seriously dowse for a well, but I believe that by trying the exercises, you'll be outdoors experiencing nature, and you will perhaps see things that you have not noticed before. You'll also begin to experience the energies of the earth.

Some people say it is already too late. We've poured so many toxic chemicals onto the surface of our globe that the drinking water in the water table is already polluted beyond repair. This may or may not be so, but dowsers know how to find a different supply, from a source that is not in the heavens, and isn't part of the water cycle: rain, to land, to creek, to lake, to evaporation, to clouds, to rain.

If you've taken chemistry at school, you know that water is a by-product in many chemical processes. One of the basic reactions is that an acid (for example, hydrochloric acid) plus a base (sodium hydroxide) makes a salt (in this case, sea salt or sodium chloride) plus water. ($HCl + NaOH = NaCl +$

H_2O.) Chemical reactions are continually taking place in the depths of our planet, where the magma at the core adds fire to the union of these chemicals. The watery by-product is turned to steam which moves rapidly away from the heat. As the steam expands it finds cracks or necks in the mantle or crust of the earth, and under pressure from below, the water cools and comes up toward the surface of the earth sometimes emerging as bubbling mineral springs or forceful geysers.

In most cases, this water, coming up through what dowsers call a dome or a blind spring, never reaches the surface, but is cut off somewhere on its journey upward by some impermeable material like clay. It then goes out at various levels in the dome, wherever there are cracks in the rock, as underground veins of water. Dowsers use the word *vein* to describe an underground fissure of water. The dome is the heart, and the veins act as blood vessels. When viewed from above, on the surface of the earth, this dome and vein structure looks like a fat round spider with an odd number of legs – often five, but I've once seen up to thirteen.

Occasionally, juvenile water actually reaches the surface of the earth. These places were called holy wells by our ancestors. In many instances these special waters bear some of the other by-products of chemical reactions. These wells are known for their mineral content. The Chalice Well at Glastonbury, in England is known for its iron rich, chalybeate water. While it looks quite clear, this water leaves a dark red stain on the rocks.

In a beautiful garden, open to all for a small maintenance fee, Chalice Well is a place of natural peace. The waters that purify, sanctify, and sometimes heal are sought by thousands of pilgrims each year. Every continent on Earth has wells of holy juvenile water that have been recognized as sacred by the indigenous peoples of those continents for millennia.

It is the juvenile water that doesn't quite reach the surface of the earth that is of interest to water dowsers who look for 'a good vein of water.' Juvenile water has never been part of the water table. The more mature water table waters can be polluted by man. Juvenile water hasn't yet been exposed to those pollutants.

In Vermont, where the Headquarters of the American Society of Dowsers is found, water dowsers look for juvenile water in veins that are between 50 and 250 feet (15–76 m) below the surface. Anything beyond 400 feet (121 m) down is considered a waste of time, but there are a few successful wells below that depth. The best place to drill is at a crossing point, where there are two intersecting veins of good potable water that, between them, will yield at least 5 gallons (19 l) a minute year' round. By 'intersecting', I don't mean that the veins are at the same depth below the surface. The veins are normally at different depths. The drill coming down from the surface intersects the two veins at different depths. If you deliberately drill on a crossing, or intersection of veins, you're doubling your odds of hitting water.

If, as I believe, being able to find these crossings of veins of juvenile water is going to be so important, how can you learn to dowse for them yourself? The best way, of course, is to spend time with a competent dowser, or to attend classes at one of the dowsing schools that deal specifically with water dowsing. Some of the dowsing related organizations mentioned on page 122, at the end of this book, offer these courses.

You can learn to dowse for water on your own, however, and there are several clues provided by nature that can help you to find at least one vein of underground juvenile water. This means that you will have to get outside into the countryside, but you may be surprised at what you'll find. Many insects choose to build their homes on veins or crossings of veins of water. Dowsers have found that ants build their hills over juvenile water. I understand that termite mounds are found over this kind of water as well. Wild bees locate the entrance of their hives over juvenile water, and if the bees swarm, the swarm will also be over juvenile water.

Many animals choose to locate the openings of their underground homes on veins of juvenile water. I have dowsed groundhog, snake, woodchuck, badger, fox and prairie dog holes, and all were over veins of water.

Deer seem to love juvenile water. Have you ever been walking through a meadow of high grass and come across a deer 'form'? The grass is all matted down from the imprint of their sleeping position. There's bound to be juvenile water underneath. During the mating season, like a dog to a fire hydrant, the buck will go around the boundaries of his territory and at various specific locations he urinates and then paws the urine into the ground. You can see these places in the autumn as circular spots of bare earth on the leafy forest floor. Game Wardens call these spots deer 'paws'. Dowsers recognize them as domes of water.

Do you have a cat? Does it have a favorite place or two in the house? The spots that cats seem to like often mark juvenile water. I slept one night in the guest bedroom of a friend of mine. His cat insisted on sleeping on the lower right-hand corner of the bed. In the morning I dowsed and found out why, the cat was drawn to spend time over a point where two veins of primary water crossed beneath the house. These intersections seem to more than double a cat's pleasure!

There are various plants that, grown in the wild, choose to take root over underground juvenile water. Juniper, the berry Caesar used to enrage his troops before battle, and now best known as the basis of gin, is one of the first larger bushes to establish itself in a pasture if the field is allowed to revert naturally to woodland. Juniper grows out from a center of bushes. Sometimes, like a doughnut, the center bush dies off, while the outer ring thrives. Juniper likes best to take root over domes of water. I've also seen vetch, a notable weed on Vermont gardens, growing in a ring over a dome, and tiny English daisies grow in circles over crossings of underground veins of water. Fairy rings of mushrooms are yet another example of a natural indication of underground water.

The hardwood trees in Vermont, given enough room, grow tall and strong with their branches growing slowly outward and upward away from the trunk. Sometimes, for no apparent reason (except that there is a vein of juvenile water directly under the junction), the branches suddenly go straight up, at ninety degrees from the branch that comes from the trunk. A tree may exhibit this ninety degree turn of branches all the way around the entire trunk. Often this tree is the monarch of the surrounding forest. Native Americans call these trees 'council trees' because council was once held under the branches. Similarly, the Anglo Saxon *moot*, or the Norse *ting*, are places of council.

Many of the observations concerning water and spots over which plants like to grow and certain animals like to spend time, were first made by a somewhat enigmatic British dowser, Guy Underwood. He spent years wandering over the British countryside in the middle of this century and wrote of his discoveries in his book, *The Pattern of the Past*. Since the publication of his book many dowsers have confirmed the connection.

Perhaps you know of a place where a natural spring comes to the surface of the earth. Alternatively, you might have noticed some animal or plant evidence on the surface of the earth, that may indicate an underground vein of water. While this water is not necessarily juvenile water, it can give you something to practice on in the following exercise.

If you are aware of any of the phenomena or places that I have described so far near you, go there. Take out your pendulum, and if you are at a sacred place this is especially important, go through the tuning-in steps, 'This is what I want to do. Can I? May I? Am I ready?' Then ask yourself, 'Is there a vein or dome that marks this target I'm looking at?' (You can insert the specific name of the plant, animal evidence, or sacred spot for the word 'target' in the previous sentence.) If the answer is yes, ask, 'Is this the Truth?' If it's still yes, proceed with the following.

Review in your mind how the pendulum reacts as you approach the target in your search position, (then in an ellipse, and into a circle when you're over the target, and then back into an ellipse as you go beyond). With your pendulum in the search position, say to yourself, 'I am looking for a vein of juvenile water,' and begin to walk slowly around your target. If everything is right so far, you should have the ellipse/circle/ellipse response at least twice as you walk around the target. This would indicate that there is one vein of juvenile water flowing under your target. If there are more of these reactions as you walk around your target, there are more veins. If there are an even number of similar responses (say six), that would indicate that you have a crossing of (three) veins. On the other hand, if you have an odd number of responses, five would be a common number here in Vermont, this would indicate that you are walking around the outside of a dome that has, in this case, five veins exiting from the dome.

In the last chapter, I said that it didn't necessarily matter which way your pendulum rotates, clockwise or counterclockwise, in the ellipse/circle/ellipse procedure. Flowing veins of underground water have a yin, or minus, charge. Perhaps you will notice that your pendulum has gone in a counterclockwise ellipse and circle, indicating the charge of the target.

Go over the vein(s) of primary water several times to get the feel of them. Try it again further away from the target. Do you still find the same number of veins?

Can you track one of them? Stand directly over the vein. With your pendulum in your search position ask, 'Which way is upstream?'

Your leading edge will take you in that direction. As you walk in that direction, continue to watch your leading edge. As the vein turns, it turns. You can follow underground pipes in this way as well.

LOOKING FOR DRINKING WATER

As I said before, I feel that looking for good drinking water is only one aspect of the world of dowsing, but in the next twenty-five years, due to the increasing pollution of our more mature surface water, the ability to find juvenile water will become the most sought after service dowsers can provide. I urge you to learn more about this. To learn to be a master water dowser takes years, lots of mistakes, and a great deal of perseverance; however, it could be a most important personal and community survival skill in the future. The following exercise has been extended to include a few tips that you can use to increase your odds of hitting good water.

First of all, when you go on a search for a well, ask for a crossing of two or more veins of juvenile water that are both potable, are less than 250 feet (76 m) down, will produce at least five gallons (19 l) of water per minute (this is more than enough for most private home usage), and one that will flow year 'round. My mother, for example, runs her house on a flow of one gallon and a half (5–6 l) per minute, but it is much safer to go for a minimum of five gallons (19 l) per minute. It gives you a reserve to draw on when you need a lot of water. Some juvenile water is full of sulphur or other foul tasting chemicals. If it's too deep, the drilling costs become prohibitive, and if the well runs dry every summer, what good is it?

Let the leading edge and triangulation techniques lead you to the wellhead where the ellipse/circle/ellipse movements of your pendulum will tell you if you are on target. Find out how many veins cross at that point. Never drill on a dome! The enormous pressure of air at the surface of the earth will push the head of the dome down until the pressure to push the water sideways is equal to the downward pressure. The end result is that you lose the water.

Dowse instead for the veins that come out of a dome. There are always an odd number of veins coming out of a dome. Best of all, look for a place where two of those veins cross each other (at different depths). Two veins crossing look like an 'X' on the surface of the earth, but one could be much closer to the surface than the other.

Now it's time to determine the depth. With your pendulum in the search position, 'Is it over 50 feet (15 m) to the top of the higher vein?' If your pendulum says yes, 'Is it over 100 (30 m)?' Yes. '150(46 m)?' No.

So you gnow (intuitively know) that it is between 100 (30 m) and 150 feet (46 m) down. Notice in the second and third questions that I left out, ' . . . feet to the top of the vein.' And in the third question, 'Is it over . . .,' and just said, '150?'

This is dowsing shorthand. Sometimes, when you are asking a lot of similar questions, dowsers shorten the question like this to save time. In the context of what was going on in the above depth questions, '150?' means, 'Is it over 150 feet to the top of the higher of the two veins of juvenile water that cross at this spot?' The higher vein is somewhere between 100 and 150 feet (30–46 m) below the surface of the earth.

If you want to get more specific as to depth, you can phrase your questions accordingly. You also could use the Zero to One Hundred Chart. When you have determined that the

Juvenile or primary water travels up from the depths of the earth through vertical cracks in the mantle called domes, RIGHT. When the water in the dome reaches an impermeable layer, if flows out as veins through smaller cracks on the side of the dome. From the dowser's point of view, BELOW, a dome and its veins look like a spider.

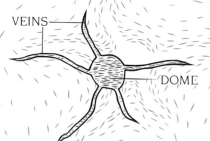

VEINS — DOME

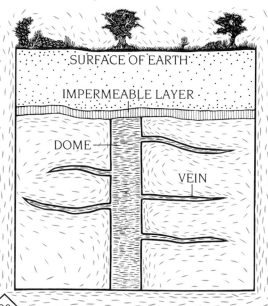

SURFACE OF EARTH

IMPERMEABLE LAYER

DOME — VEIN

vein is between 100 and 150 feet (30–46 m) down, the chart can represent the numbers 100 to 200 instead of 0 to 100. With your pendulum on the hinge of the fan, ask the question, 'How many feet over 100 is it to the top of the higher of the two veins that cross at this spot?' The leading edge starting on 50 will move counterclockwise to, say, 36. So the entire depth to the top of the first vein is 136 feet (41 m).

Using this same technique, you can find the depth to the top of the deeper of the two veins. Your well driller will have to go just slightly beyond this depth.

A water dowser must also be able to determine the potential gallons per minute the home owner can expect from this well. This is done using the same 'is it greater than/less than' technique we used in the depth section. Start with one gallon, two, three. . . . When you get to ten, go up by tens until you get a no. Then work the exact gallonage by ones, as in the final depth example. You can also use the Zero to One Hundred Chart.

You're now ready to drive a stake into the ground to indicate to the well driller where to drill. Put the tip of the stake into the ground. 'Is this the best place for the driller to put the drill bit?' Yes. 'Is this the Truth?' Yes. You've got it!

One final thing. I would still urge you to connect with a good local dowser if you can find one. Try the directories of the national dowsing organization in your country, or if you are in Fountain International, contact your nearest Fountain Group. See Dowsing Related Organizations and Publications in the back of this book. Also, go to one of the schools that deal with water dowsing in your area. Remember, more and more dowsers are interested in using dowsing for things other than water, so if you decide to take a dowsing class, make sure that you understand exactly what the workshop is going to cover.

So go for it. Like all dowsing activities, water dowsers don't succeed every time. You won't either. But if you can develop the skills of being able to find clean drinking water at least 85 percent of the time, as many competent water dowsers can, then you will have a valuable service to offer, especially in the next fifty years or so.

OTHER PRACTICAL SUGGESTIONS

As a dowser, you can look for, and find anything you can think of. In the United States, many municipalities regularly use L rods (another dowsing tool discussed in chapter 5) to find underground pipes or electrical wires. It's interesting to note that, generally, these municipalities don't consider this to be dowsing. They explain that some of their employees seem to be able to 'work' L rods quite successfully. The important thing is that L rods are effective tools to use to find underground pipes in parts of the city where the maps have been lost. You can try the same thing using map dowsing with your pendulum.

Some dowsers use a pendulum when they're prospecting for crystals, minerals and fossils. I sometimes use my pendulum to find out how many people there will be at a meeting or workshop. How about using your pendulum to tell you when that corn you're cooking is cooked to perfection?

You might want to try to use dowsing to find animals or birds when you are walking through the woods. Or you might be spinning for trout at the edge of a deep woodland pool.

You know that there is a monster trout in there. The first cast is the most important. So where is the big fish? You can use the lure as a pendulum on the end of your fishing pole to show you with its leading edge the exact direction you must cast in the pool for that big one.

Several of my friends have become quite good at dowsing where there are leaks in underground pipes, or places where there are blockages. First they map out where the pipe runs, then they walk along that line looking for leaks or blocks. You can try this in the next exercise.

Find an underground pipe near your home. With your pendulum, using the leading edge, find out where it runs. Now ask your pendulum where there are joints in the pipe, or places where two different pieces of pipe come together. Walk along the pipe with your pendulum in the search position. Every time you approach a joint in the pipe, your pendulum will go from your search position to a clockwise circle. When the pendulum is going in a full circle, you will be directly over a joint in the pipe. You could make a map of your results to use whenever you need to check the pipe again.

Looking for a leak or blockage is the same process as looking for a joint in pipes. As you can dowse to tell plumbers where to dig and how far down (using the technique I explained on page 91), your skill can save people a lot of money.

ANCIENT SACRED PLACES

Many readers of this book will know of an ancient sacred spot near where they live. Who were the indigenous people in your neighbourhood? How did they mark their sacred spaces? There are many sacred sites in every country in which this book is published. From Aboriginal sacred springs and glyphs, through enormous effigy mounds (of animals, humans, and 'space' people), and underground chambers oriented toward the Solstice or Equinox, to stone medicine wheels and circles, the peoples of this Earth have indicated holy places in many different ways. Because these places are holy, it is important to approach them with the right attitude. If you expect to learn from such a place, you must come with respect in your heart.

It is possible to learn all kinds of things about sacred space using dowsing techniques. The first thing that you can look for is juvenile water. The bigger the sacred space, the more water there is likely to be. Perhaps you will find a dome and may find it is in a special area of the sacred space. Underground water is yin, or negative, and has been written about in the dowsing literature since the 1930s.

In the 1920s an Englishman named Alfred Watkins wrote a book called *The Old Straight Track*, in which he told of finding alignments of ancient sacred spots throughout England. These markers ranged from standing stones and megalithic rings, through holy wells, and Bronze Age round burial barrows and Iron Age hill forts, to the spires of Anglo Saxon churches and Gothic cathedrals. Straight lines across the country linked together by holy places are called ley lines. Steeple chasing, or riding on horseback in a straight line from one steeple to the next, 'come hell or high water', is a remnant of the ancient awareness of ley lines. A ley line is defined as an alignment of at least five sacred sites, each of which has juvenile water under it. Ley lines are found on nearly every continent on Earth (I don't know of any on Antarctica).

These ley lines are sometimes accompanied by a beam of yang or positive energy, called an energy ley. Six to eight foot (1–2 m) wide beams of yang energy run like meridians or capillaries all over the surface of the earth, carrying nourishment in various forms to the countryside and to the inhabitants of the area. At any ancient place of sanctity, there will be at least one of these energy leys, and it will run along the major axis of the site.

If you live near a known sacred site, go there with respect, and try dowsing for an energy ley. Ask your pendulum for the position of the nearest one. (You can ask to look for the energy ley closest to your home, perhaps by dowsing over a map, but you may have to travel far to find it.) Walk to the edge of the energy ley. What does it feel like? Can you notice any reaction or physical sensation within yourself? Go through to the other edge, usually 6 to 8 feet (1–2 m) away, turn around, and dowse there as well.

The energy runs like a river, and it has a definite direction of flow. You can find this by asking, 'Which way is downstream?' Your leading edge will point the way.

The energy power center of the site is at a place where the juvenile water (domes, veins) and the energy leys cross. This is a major place to locate at any sacred site. Indeed, some sites have more than one power center.

In dowsing the edge of an energy ley, you've gone from the physical to the non-physical, from dowsing for tangible targets to dowsing for intangible ones. You can see a ley line through its alignment with other sacred sites, either on a map or on the ground. But you can't touch, see, hear, smell, or taste an energy ley, or get a needle to move on a scientific instrument in response to it. Many dowsers intuitively know that they exist, however.

As I approach a power center with my pendulum, the first thing I notice is that the hair at the bottom of my neck begins to tingle. Then, as I get closer and closer to the exact center, my pendulum not only goes from an ellipse to a circle, but its speed of rotation increases until it is almost parallel with the surface of the Earth! This increase in velocity is like a scale. The greater the velocity, the more energies there are to work with at that particular power center.

Remember, there are as many ways of looking at a sacred site with a pendulum as there are pendulum users. Everybody sees these intangible targets slightly differently. Go with how you are 'seeing' it, dowsing it. Your intuitive experience can teach you a lot.

If this particular aspect of dowsing is of interest to you, I have written extensively on it in my book, *Spiritual Dowsing*, which also discusses further uses of the pendulum in the field of healing. See the 'Books To Read Section' on page 120 at the end of this book.

In this chapter we've focused primarily on juvenile water, on what it is, how to find it, and how to dowse for it. I briefly mentioned other outdoor uses of this ancient craft and the rest of the chapter was devoted to using dowsing at ancient sacred sites and looking at the earth energies that are found there.

As you grow in your dowsing skills, you will discover other uses for dowsing out of doors; however, I'd urge you to gain as much experience as you can locating juvenile, or primary, water. I seriously believe that there won't be a more valuable skill to possess in the years to come.

CHAPTER 5

OTHER DOWSING TOOLS

Before we go on to discuss other kinds of dowsing tools, it might be helpful to consider the various kinds of pendulums available. While a hexagonal nut on the end of a length of thread will do quite nicely for many applications, to use charts, the pendulum must have a point on the end – like that on the one provided with this book.

Perhaps one of the more interesting variations is the pendulum with a 'witness chamber', a small chamber inside the pendulum into which the dowser can place a sample of the material sought. If looking for oil, one would put some high grade crude oil in it. If looking for a lost child, one might use strands of hair taken from their hair brush. Some dowsers feel that this 'witness' helps them focus their intent. (My own feeling is that if you feel that it will, then it will. The converse is also true.)

Dowsers use all kinds of pendulums. Some feel that quartz or crystal makes a better one, others swear by wood. Some prefer a squat and heavy shape. Others like them to be long, thin, and relatively light. I remember one of my more successful pendulums was a rock tied on the end of a dandelion stem!

Technically, a pendulum is a balanced weight on the end of a string, but in practice the variations are legion, and ultimately dowsers must decide for themselves which one works best.

The pendulum isn't the only dowsing device you can use. There are four main types or classes of dowsing tools, of which the pendulum is but one. The other three are Y rods, bobbers, and L rods. We'll look at them all, and in the process, go through some exercises to acquaint you with their functions.

These hands are holding the Y rod in the search position. Notice that the hands are holding the rod thumbs out. The Y rod can be held with your thumbs pressed against the rod — or not — whichever is more comfortable.

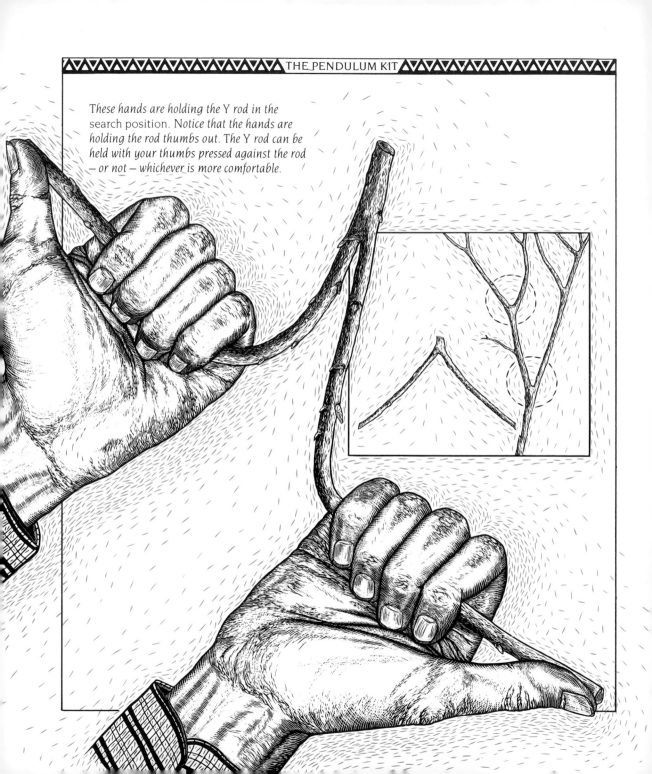

THE Y ROD

The general public is probably more familiar with the Y rod than the pendulum, as an archetypal dowsing tool. The old forked stick of apple wood has been used for hundreds of years to find water. I live in New England, in the northeastern part of the United States, and here the Y rod is the dowsing tool of choice for most old-time dowsers. Some say that only apple wood will work. Others swear by willow. I've found that any pliable forked stick of young green wood will work for me, and when it does, it is impossible to hold in the *search position* when I am over the target.

To try the Y rod yourself, go out and find a tree with branches that are as thick as your little finger. Among the branches, look for a fork, or Y, that is well balanced. Don't pick a Y where one of the arms comes out at ninety degrees from the other. The two branches should separate evenly from where they join each other. Cut the branch off at about 2 inches (5 cm) from the point where the two arms join together towards the trunk of the tree. The arms themselves can be about 18 inches (46 cm) long.

There are only two positions for the Y rod — search position and here (this is the point you're looking for). The search position is assumed by grabbing the arms with your hands, palms up and thumbs outward. Hold the Y rod with the tip pointing upward. You'll gnow (intuitively know) the search position when it feels like you are at a balance point between the Y rod flipping backwards hitting your face, or forwards, and snapping towards the ground. In the United States, most Y rod dowsers find that when reacting the rod goes away from their chest towards the ground. In Britain, many dowsers find that it comes backwards, towards them (they use a Y rod with shorter arms so it won't hit them in the face). As far as I can tell, as with the various possible signals with a pendulum, it is personal preference (or the preference of the teacher) that decides which way the rod goes.

Let's try to feel the Y rod work for you. Take a long piece of string, and put it on the floor stretched out in a straight line from right to left in front of you. Stand up, and hold the Y rod in the search position (thumbs out). Tell your rod, 'I want you to go down when I walk over this string, and I want you to point directly at the string.'

Walk towards the string and notice that before you even get there, you can feel the stick pulling in your hands. Hold on tightly to the stick. The rod will twist to the here position. You won't be able to hold it. Sometimes the bark twists right off in your hands!

OK. *If it doesn't work the first time, try it again several times, focusing on what you're asking the stick to do. If it still doesn't go down, like a recalcitrant pendulum, you need to show it how you want it to go. Walk over the string again, only this time, make it go down as you walk over the string. Do this several times. Impress upon the rod and yourself that this is the response that you are looking for.*

Now try it again without forcing it to go down. You may only feel a little pull the first time. Try holding your arms high above your head with the rod in the search position. *This seems to make the Y rod much more sensitive. Don't particularly look at it; feel it.*

If it still doesn't work, you have two options. You can either do this exercise each day for a week, and by then you'll probably have it, or you can forget the Y rod for a while, and try the bobber or the L rods. Not all tools work for all dowsers.

In terms of the direction of pull for the Y rod, for two reasons I prefer it to go away from my face. First of all, I have been snapped in the nose by a Y rod, and it hurts! Secondly, I find it useful to have it go away from me as the rod can then not only show *here*, but also, it can be used to show direction. This is done, for example, when you're lost in the woods. 'In which direction is my car?' Holding the Y rod in the *search position* turn slowly in a circle. Like an arm snaking out in the correct direction, the Y rod will go down when it is pointing towards your car.

Given my belief in the imminent and massive pollution of the Earth's water system, I feel it is imperative for as many of us as possible to learn how, in addition to the other areas of dowsing in which we might be involved, to be able to find good potable water. The Y rod is an excellent tool for this. When looking for a spot to drill a well, the Y rod's particular response of pointing

Made by cutting a limber switch from a tree, or by using a fishing pole, a bobber is held by the thinner end with one or both hands depending on the weight and length of the tool. The heavier tip of the bobber responds yes, *by moving up and down, and* no, *swinging from side to side.*

directly down towards the ground gives the dowser a distinct point on which to begin. Y rods can be made of different materials — apple, willow, cherry, and even plastic. Take your choice.

THE BOBBER

The bobber is a tool used primarily by water and oil dowsers and it takes several forms. The most common one is made from a fishing pole (without the reel) held by the wrong end, or the tip. To make your own and learn to use it, practice this exercise.

Go outside and cut yourself a switch from a tree by the side of a field or country road. Cut one about 3 or 4 feet (1 m) long. Hold it in front of you with either one hand or both hands on the thinner end. Have the tip pointing slightly upwards.

The yes response is up and down, like the way people nod their heads to indicate 'yes'. No is side to side, as people shake their heads 'no'. Try it. 'Show me yes.' If it doesn't respond, bounce it up and down to get it going. 'This is yes.' Then ask for no. The bobber should stop the up and down motion, and move from side to side.

If you know where the pipe that brings your water into the house is located, picture in your mind's eye where that would be on the outside of your house. Go to that point outside with your bobber in the search position, holding the thinner end and with the tip pointing away from you and slightly up.

Walk towards the underground pipe. As you approach the pipe, the bobber will start to bob, and the closer you get, the more it will bob. It will reach its maximum movement when you are directly over the pipe. Walk beyond, and see the bobbing diminish. It's the same principle as the pendulum going from your search position, to an ellipse, to a circle over the target, then back to an ellipse as you go beyond, and finally back into your search position.

Now go back and stand directly over the pipe. Let's determine the depth of the pipe — from the surface of the earth to the top of the pipe. Start the bobber in an up and down motion. (Let's say that the pipe was 4½ feet (1.3 m) down) 'I want to gnow (intuitively know) the depth of this pipe.' Starting with any downswing, or downward bob of the rod count one bob for each foot. 'Is it more than 1 foot (0.3 m) below the surface of the earth? 2 feet? 3? 4? 5?' At the count of 5, the bobber will stop going up and down, and will start moving from side to side. So you dowse that it is between the last number you counted, and the one before.

Remember the question, 'Is it more than . . .' The bobber said no at 5 and so your water pipe will be between 4 and 5 feet (1−1.5 m) down. With it again bobbing up and down, 'Is it more than 4 feet 2 inches? 4 inches? 6 inches?' Again the bobber goes from side to side. 'So is it 4 feet 6 inches (1.3 m) down?' the bobber nods yes.

If you can't locate your water pipe, any other pipe or cable will do. Perhaps you can dowse the distance to the floor above or below you. Do it to the nearest inch or centimetre.

Quite a while ago, at an American Society Of Dowsers Annual Convention, I met an Australian dowser who used a wood saw as a bobber! It really worked well for him. He would hold it with both hands at the tip of the blade, and as he approached a vein of water, that saw started bobbing so violently that I thought it would jump out of his hands. Of course the saw only allows one motion: up and down. You can't get the *no* response. (You must develop a technique of devising questions that can only be answered, yes.)

In the United States, dowsers who look for oil or water using the bobber call themselves doodlebugs, and they call their tool a Florida bobber. The bobber is a very useful device for determining depth or the answer to any other query involving numbers. And the doodlebugs swear by it for oil.

L RODS

The final tool in the dowsers' bag of tricks is a pair of L rods. These are 'L'-shaped coat hanger wires in sleeves made from good plastic straws.

I suggest that you make yourself two of them (L rods are mostly used in pairs). Get two identical coat hangers of very thick wire. With a pair of pliers, cut each hanger at the point where the hook is connected. Cut the hook and one arm off at the point just above the first turn. What you're left with is one short arm and a long one that bends out into an 'L'. Cut a plastic drinking straw an inch or so shorter than the short arm. Some fast food restaurant straws work very well as they are exceptionally wide. Slide the straw up that arm, and make sure that the arm swings freely in the straw. Make a smaller L at the end of the shorter arm, running parallel with the longer arm on the other end of the straw. This will hold the straw on. MOST IMPORTANT: Also bend an inch or so of the tip of the longer end all the way around to form a ring. This will be of some help if you accidentally jab someone!

Go to the underground water pipe you were working on with the bobber. The search position with L rods always reminds me of Billy the Kid with his six-guns out in the ready to fire position. Have your arms bent at the elbows, and lightly holding the straws so none of your hand touches the wire hanger, have the longer arms pointing directly away from you, parallel with each other. This is the search position.

You will notice that if you twist your wrists, the rods will swing in and cross to make an 'X' or swing out. It's relatively easy to do, so make sure that your need for a particular answer doesn't cause your wrists to twist unintentionally. Always be aware of what your wrists are doing as you work with the L rods and try not to clench your fists.

Walk towards the underground pipe and say, 'I want these L rods to go out when I come to the underground pipe, and I want my hands to be directly over the pipe when the arms of the L rod are fully extended in opposition to each other.'

Perhaps the rods just hung in your hands and didn't do anything when you crossed the pipe. Try it a few more times. Hold the tips of the rods up to the point where, if you lifted them any more, they would fall down to the side. This is the most sensitively balanced position of the L rods.

If you still have no luck, as with my advice for other recalcitrant tools, you have to show the rods what you want them to do. Get your rods in the search position. Walk up to the place where you know the pipe is. As you approach the spot, twist your wrists outward.

L rods can be made by cutting two substantial wire coat hangers as shown, BELOW. Create two 'L's by bending the wires out to make right angles. A drinking straw on the shorter end serves as a sleeve, but is not absolutely necessary. Some dowsers prefer L rods without sleeves.

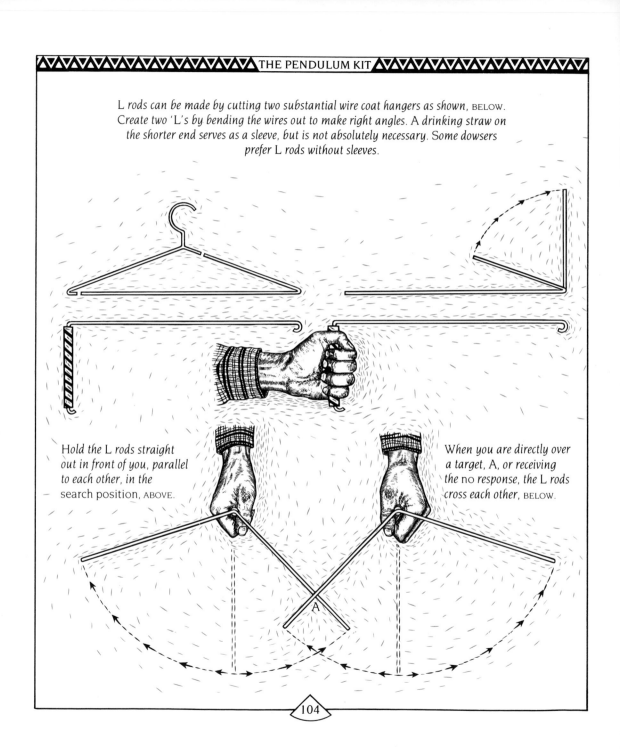

Hold the L rods straight out in front of you, parallel to each other, in the search position, ABOVE.

When you are directly over a target, A, or receiving the no response, the L rods cross each other, BELOW.

A

That's right, make the rods move! Do this several times as you reinforce what you are doing by saying things like, 'I'm approaching this pipe, and when I get closer I want you (the L rods) to go out like this' (bend your wrists).

Once you get the feel of this movement, tell your rods that you want them to cross inwards to make an X when you cross the pipe. The center of the X marks the pipe. If it's working correctly, the rods will seem to cross by themselves as you come up to the target.

For most users of the L rods, yes is open arms, no is crossed arms, or the X position, and the search position is parallel arms.

When I was in the army, I remember being posted to the Language School at the Presidio of Monterey in California. As I arrived in the middle of a language cycle, I was temporarily despatched, with several other Privates, to dismantling obsolete electrical gear into its component parts. During one of our breaks, the subject of dowsing came up. My mother had taught me to look for underground water pipes about five years before, so that when I saw a standpipe in the middle of a field, I took it upon myself to find out where the pipe came from that brought the water.

I made some L rods from the thick, coated wire we had taken out of an electronic console, and went out to find the pipe. We were stationed quite near the edge of the camp, and it was clear that the water had to come from the center of the Presidio where most of the other buildings were located. However, when I walked on that side of the standpipe, I got no reaction at all; but, as I walked around the standpipe, I felt the familiar pull of the rods in exactly the opposite direction from where I had expected it to be! This couldn't be right. My companions, who were skeptical about dowsing anyway, were now convinced that it really didn't work.

I remember puzzling about it when I went to bed that night. The next day, when I got to the electronic demolition project, I pulled out the L rods, and tried again. The pipe seemed to be coming from a building next to the perimeter fence – in totally the wrong direction. I followed the direction of the underground pipe until I came to the edge of that building. Right there at my feet I could see the pipe going into the foundation wall! I think I got a convert or two that day. The technique I used is explained in the following exercise.

To find direction, hold just one L rod out in the search position, and say to yourself something like, 'Where's the nearest street light?' Keep your L rod in the search position, but turn your body around in a tight circle. When you come to the direction that the nearest street light will be found, the tip of the L rod seems to stick to that direction. As you continue to turn, the L rod tip will remain pointing towards the nearest street light. This technique is also good for, 'Where is North?', or, 'I'm lost on the mountains, where's the most accessible first aid hut?' Let your intuition, via the L rods, show you the way. No matter which way you turn and twist, the L rod just seems to stick to the right direction.

You can also use L rods to show you the way any particular underground feature runs. Do you know if your water pipe comes straight out of your house, or if it leaves at an angle? Ask the rods to show you the direction in which the pipe runs. Walk towards the pipe with your rods in the search position. As you get near, notice how they start turning out. When the arms are out opposite each other, you are not only directly over the pipe, but the arms show both directions of the pipe. Try approaching the pipe at an oblique angle. Notice how one arm goes out a long way, and the other goes out only a little, thus showing you the line of the pipe.

Each one of the dowsing tools is better for a particular kind of dowsing than the other. The pendulum is convenient and quick to answer *yes/no* questions. The Y rod is good at locating a specific point. The bobber is good for gauging depth, and the L rods are especially useful when trying to determine the direction or flow of an underground feature. However, you will also find that you can use any one tool for all your dowsing needs. I have a friend who is an excellent water dowser. She also practices many other kinds of dowsing and uses only her pendulum.

Ultimately, it doesn't really matter which dowsing tool you use. The most important thing is that whatever tool you are using, it should seem to work for you. You'll find that you establish a kind of rapport with the tool that you're using. When you are dowsing well, you are relaxed, but the tool feels as if it were living. The pendulum seems to move on its own, and spins around in an excited fashion. The Y rod has a life of its own, and at times reacts unexpectedly. As you approach your target, almost as if it were sensing that nearness, it begins to quiver in your hands. Then, with an increasing sense of pull, it bounds down to indicate the exact location. The bobber twitches and jumps in its own inimitable way and I find that it is an amazingly responsive instrument. The L rods too, have a way of moving on their own. Experienced dowsers hold the tips down in a heavy wind, but the rods, as they move out, seem to go uphill!

Getting back to pendulums, have you been doing the basic exercises recently? Please try them now. Get your pendulum out, and begin in your search position. Then, 'Show me yes, *this is positive, this is active, this is yang, this is yes.'* Then, 'This is no, *this is negative, this is receptive, this is yin, this is no.'*

CHAPTER 6

CONCLUSION

T his final chapter brings together topics that are an integral part of dowsing but have not yet been discussed: the history of this ancient art; how science classifies dowsing; how dowsing relates to science. There are also some suggestions of further directions you might want to explore, covering the intangible world of thought forms, and the less physical world of deviceless dowsing.

HISTORY OF DOWSING

The roots of dowsing can be traced back through the mists of ancient time. There are bits and pieces of evidence that point to several people who could lay claim to have originated dowsing. Some say that pictoglyphs on the walls of the Tassili Caves in southern Algeria in Africa bear the earliest evidence. These caves have human-like figures that have been dated to 6,000 years before Christ. One of the figures holds a forked stick in what we would call the *search position*. Over 2,000 years before Christ, a Chinese emperor named Yu, was not only a dowser, but according to some, went on an expedition to the east and traveled through what is now the western part of the United States and west coast of Mexico!

Perhaps the best source of information on the ancient art of dowsing is a reference (much quoted by dowsers) found in the Bible. At one point on their exodus through the Sinai, the people who had followed Moses into the desert had run out of grain and fruit and water, and understandably, there was much

unrest. The Lord told Moses (we call this channelling today), 'Take the rod, and assemble the congregation, you and Aaron your brother, and tell the rock before their eyes to yield its water.'

So Moses and Aaron got the people together, and Moses stood up and said to them, 'Hear now, you rebels; shall we bring forth water for you out of this rock?' And Moses lifted up his hand and struck the rock with his rod twice, and water came forth abundantly ...' (Bible, Revised Standard. Numbers 20:8–11) As it was mentioned first by the Lord, the 'rod' here seems to be more than just a walking staff; it was apparently a very special piece of wood. Moses had used this same rod in Egypt quite effectively in his dealings with the pharaoh. Events like this are often called 'miracles'. A miracle, according to Webster's Dictionary, is defined in part as 'an event or effect in the physical world deviating from the laws of nature.' Using modern scientific definitions of the laws of nature, dowsing is a miracle. And Moses was a dowser.

More recent historical evidence of dowsing comes from the persecutions and burnings for witchcraft during the Middle Ages and the Renaissance. The last witch was put to death in Calvinist Scotland in 1728 AD. Indigenous people throughout Europe had used dowsing as one of their tools to heal themselves and others. Their ability to find water was so important that it just couldn't be stamped out. Water dowsers survived. But those who used it for healing and personal spiritual work were brutally suppressed. According to feminist researchers like Monica Sjöö and Starhawk, 9,000,000 deaths can be attributed to the Church and the Inquisition during this period. British historian Ronald Hutton, from the University of Bristol, disputes this figure and has concluded that it is closer to 60,000. Perhaps there were only 60,000 deaths, but the end result was the same – the intuitive consciousness in Europe was dealt a severe blow, and the old ways, including dowsing, died in the hearts of well over 9,000,000 people as a result.

Author Chris Bird begins his history of dowsing, *The Divining Hand*, in the mid–1600s, with the story of a Frenchman, Martine de Bertereau, who successfully dowsed over 150 coal mines, and was rewarded with life imprisonment. This is a story of how dowsing has benefitted science but not the dowser! Over the years dowsing techniques have been used to locate many metals essential for the machines of science. Like the water dowsers, the metal dowsers of Europe became so valuable that the Church couldn't suppress them either.

When I first joined the American Society of Dowsers in the late 1960s, the average participant who attended the Annual Convention was a 65 year old male. There are many more women now. Even with this early male dominance, there are several women who have made a name for themselves in the dowsing field, and one of them is Evelyn Penrose. Born in Cornwall, in England, from a long line of dowsers, Evelyn moved to Canada, and in 1931 she was employed by the government of British Columbia as a water and mineral diviner. She had a success rate of 90 percent, and the stories of her finding water for farmers and ranchers during droughts are legion. Not content with her success in Canada, in the late 1940s, she went to New South Wales in Australia, and was very helpful there finding water, again for drought struck ranchers and farmers.

Various societies were established in Europe in the 1920s and 1930s, and the British Society of Dowsers was among them. It wasn't until 1958 that a group of water dowsers got together in Danville, Vermont in the United States. They later formed the American Society of Dowsers, and have been holding gatherings and conventions, and local chapter meetings all over the United States ever since. Information on specific organizations is found on page 122 in the Dowsing Related Organizations and Publications Section.

The terms that are used to describe this ancient art echo its roots; how it was used then. Dowsers are also called 'diviners', and there is something divine in the connections that are made through the use of dowsing. Dowsers are sometimes called 'water witches'. This is a clear indication of where dowsing comes from. It comes from the witch tradition, the goddess tradition, the female, intuitive side of our heritage.

DOWSING AND SCIENCE

When one explores the literature, it is clear that there have been very few successful results of scientific examinations into dowsing. In 1906, Professor

Julius Wertheimer conducted what has become known as the old standard scientific test for dowsers: on the ground in front of the dowser are three pipes; each is connected to a water source. The question is, 'Which one has water running through it right now?' As with most subsequent tests of this nature, the (apparently well qualified) dowsers failed.

K.W. Merrylees, a past President of the British Society of Dowsers, felt sure enough of his dowsing skills that he allowed himself to become part of a test set up in the early 1970s to see if dowsers could find unexploded World War II bombs in an area of north London. Merrylees and his fellow dowsers didn't do better than chance.

Bill Lewis, a master dowser from Wales, whom I've had the pleasure to work with near his home town of Abergavenny, is known throughout Britain for his skills as a dowser. When he was working with Paul Devereux on The Dragon Project at the Rollright Stone Circle, just north of Oxford, they began talking about radioactivity at sacred sites. Bill pulled out his pendulum, and pointed out a ring of clover within the circle. He told Paul that he would find increased radioactivity there. As there were two geiger counters at the site (one belonged to Bill), this was immediately checked out and confirmed! And yet, when Bill was asked to do an electronics version of the standard three water pipe routine – Bill did it with 25 electronic circuits and was asked which were switched on, and which were off – he didn't achieve results better than chance.*

Fran Farrelly is a Trustee of the American Society of Dowsers, and a highly regarded dowser from Florida. She is one of the most respected female dowsers in the United States today. Fran has done work for Stanford Research International in Menlo Park, California. Perhaps the best known Stanford work is in the area of remote viewing, dowsing to discover an unknown place or event. While many subjects could 'see' a given scene with an amazing degree of accuracy, most could not tell where the scene was. Fran felt that perhaps dowsers could use their map-dowsing skills to find a location, so she conducted a series of experiments entitled Project Search through the pages

* From: Page 105 & 108, Dowsing, The Psi Connection, Francis Hitchings

112

of the ASD Digest, asking dowsers of all skill levels to try to locate various objects on a map.

The results were less than inspiring. In her second experiment, for example, she asked ASD members to locate the point on a map of St. Petersburg, Florida, where two home-bound elderly ladies lived. Using a grid overlay of 400 squares (20 across and 20 up and down), only three of 202 dowser respondents correctly marked the exact square of the two ladies' home.

While some experiments had better results than others, on the whole, all the tests together showed that dowsers achieved results that were no better than those determined by chance.

Why would all of these very competent dowsers risk their reputations in their attempt to prove scientifically that dowsing works, unless they *gnew* (intuitively knew) that they had achieved successful, positive dowsing results in the past?

And yet, time and again, when dowsing is exposed to the light of science, it doesn't seem to work. There are some exceptions to this statement. Dr. Zaboj V. Harvalik, a respected professor of physics at the University of Arkansas, and later an adviser to the United States Army's Advanced Concepts Materials Agency in Alexandria, Virginia, is a special case. For many years, Dr. Harvalik published the results of his experiments in the ASD Digest, many being done in the back yard of his home in Lorton, Virginia. Without going into great detail, he was able to create electromagnetic fields by putting certain frequencies into the earth. He found that 90 percent of the people he tested were able to detect a change of less than half a gamma unit. One German dowser in particular, Wilhelm De Boer, could detect changes in the magnetic field one billion times weaker than the earth's relatively weak field! Unfortunately, Dr. Harvalik's work forms part of a very meager group of successful scientific tests on dowsers. It's the exception to the general rule.

I have my Master's degree in 'Sacred Space'. This was an interdisciplinary degree, in which I studied how sacred enclosures around the world were constructed during the time of the pre-Protestant Reformation. These sites vary enormously in appearance. Compare the Great Pyramid in Egypt; Chartres, a Gothic cathedral east of Paris; Stonehenge; native American effigy mounds like the Serpent Mound in Adams County, in the state of Ohio in the United States; and Angkor Wat in Thailand. While they may look quite different from each other, these holy places share some interesting similarities. They're all built on power centers; they are constructed using certain geometrical principles, called sacred geometry; and the site is oriented towards an important celestial (usually solar or lunar, and rarely stellar) event. This last determinant involves the study of ancient astronomy that is called archaeoastronomy.

These three common factors — power centers, sacred geometry and archaeoastronomy — seem to work as enhancers with things like incense, chanting, drumming, and other spiritual practices. They enhance the possibility of increasing awareness of our intuitive side. It's like a well-built violin. Everything is done to enhance the 'sound' although, in this case, it's not sound that is enhanced but spiritual awareness.

A scientific laboratory is an entirely different kind of space. It is set up to enhance the rational and the linear instead of the intuitive. Everything is done to remove the subjective, and remove any possibility of an unpredicted reaction. No wonder dowsing doesn't do well in such an environment! When the intuition is completely surrounded and controlled by rational forces, it is reasonable to assume that it won't work very well.

To me, trying to dowse in a completely controlled scientific experiment feels like being that little dot of dark in the sea of light that makes up half of the 'tennis ball' yin/yang symbol (page 63). The dowser is the little dark dot, completely surrounded by the light of science, and cut off from his or her dark, intuitive side. Yes, it is possible to have the intuitive work under these conditions, but not probable.

An ideal environment in which a dowser's intuitive side can work is sacred space. That's where Bill Lewis' radioactive clover patch was found. A scientific laboratory is the antithesis of sacred space.

Perhaps a better question might be, 'Why do the dowsing skills that we intuitively 'know' work for us in the real world suddenly disappear when we use the scientific method to convince others of dowsing's validity?

One of the basic tenets of the scientific method is predicated on consistent repeatability. I should be able to design an experiment so that anyone else on Earth, given the same equipment and procedures, will get the same results. Dowsing just doesn't work that way. It isn't 100 percent correct all the time. It isn't always repeatable.

I talked with Project Search Director Fran Farrelly about her series of experiments. Aside from feeling disappointed in the results, she went on to say, 'I don't think dowsers can meet the criteria of the scientific method at this time. This is especially true when one brings in the issue of repeatability.'

I trust that you've discovered that the thing that most gets in the way of the dowser is the dowser. As individuals, our expectations, needs and the specific level of consciousness that we bring to the dowsing experience can all influence the response. Take Quantum Mechanics; Werner Heisenberg, in his principle of uncertainty, speaks about the impossibility of separating the observer from the experiment. This view translates well to the competent dowser failing in the presence of a coolly objective, perhaps slightly antagonistic scientific observer. The observer does interact with the experiment, and unfortunately, not all of the parts of the experiment are working together.

Part of the dilemma comes from the reality that twentieth century man (but not necessarily twentieth century woman) has given away his right to define ultimate reality, what is true, to scientists. Scientists have become the priests of the twentieth century. For some, scientists define reality. If you can't taste it, see it, touch it, smell it, hear it, or get it to move a needle on a dial, it doesn't exist. If Science says it isn't so, it isn't so.

The exploration of our intuition, and what Carl Jung calls the unconscious, or land of the archetypes, and dowsing, all require a different approach, that doesn't deny the validity of science, but seeks to use both science and intuition. Not just left brain focused analytical humanism, but also the intuitive, creative, spiritual, expansive right brain activities as well.

Techniques that had helped indigenous people everywhere to personally experience the intuitive and the spiritual have been suppressed for a thousand years. We're all babies in the field of dowsing. In our present stage of development it's about as relevant for a scientist to put most dowsers to a scientific test as it would be to apply Olympic equestrian judging standards to a nine-year old girl in her first year of riding school. The art of twentieth century dowsing is still in its infancy.

Dowsing as a skill, isn't anti-scientific. As a matter of fact, it demands a rational approach to developing the right question, that any scientist would approve of. It is time, however, for scientists to take another approach, and start working with, instead of experimenting on, gifted dowsers. It is this marriage of the scientific and the intuitive, the objective with the subjective, that will yield the best results.

THOUGHT FORMS AND DOWSING

Thought has form.

Test this concept for yourself. Get out your favorite dowsing device, and draw an 'imaginary' line with your finger a short distance in front of you. Now dowse for that line as if you were looking for a vein of water. The dowsing responses should be identical.

One of the most simple examples of the power of thought occurs when the dowser is more interested in obtaining a specific answer than in hearing the truth. In this case, the dowser's *own* thought forms get in the way. We have discussed this earlier on several occasions. Wanting a certain answer causes you to get that answer.

Thought forms can be created in many different ways. In the United States, every year in mid-September, eight or nine hundred people converge on Danville, Vermont, for the Annual Convention of the American Society of Dowsers. Most of the outdoor practice occurs on the Danville Town Green. Over the years, thousands of dowsers have looked for water there.

Dowsing isn't *always* correct. (I am very skeptical of anyone who tells me that they're always accurate, or that they've never missed a water well or energy line.) As they are learning, many beginners dowse veins of water that just aren't there. So I believe that many dowsers end up planting some thought forms on Danville Town Green whether they've actually found veins of underground water or not. While the Green has quite a few true veins of underground water, it is now also loaded with all kinds of bogus thought form veins that dowsers have placed there, thinking that they were true veins.

Anger can create very strong thought forms. Let's say you have a fight with your partner, and then decide that it is time to make up. If you find yourself in the same space where you had the fight, like a dark cloud, the anger will still be hanging there, and it will work against your attempt at reconciliation. Burning fresh, dried sage, and carrying it to the four corners of the room while you focus your intent to clean up the room of all negativity, will help to remove those angry thought forms – and make it a much more pleasant place to be. (Incidentally, sage works well in rooms where people have been ill.)

For a pantomimist, thought forms are very real. A friend of mine, Rob Mermin, a student of Marcel Marceau, found out about the 'reality' of thought forms the hard way. On one occasion, while he was on a bare stage, he created a room with his gestures, and proceeded to do his act within that room. Without thinking, he accidentally walked straight into one of the 'walls' he had created, and was knocked backwards onto his rear end!

Thought forms can hang around for a long time. At one time, I was in central England following one of the ley lines (alignment of holy sites) that runs through Arbor Low, a megalithic recumbent stone circle near Buxton in Derbyshire, and a famous ley center. (With a recumbent stone circle, there is no evidence that the stones were ever standing upright.) The ley line I was following did not have an energy ley (see page 93) flowing concurrently with it. Of the thirty or more ley lines that are claimed to cross through Arbor Low (some claim even more), I found only four energy leys.

But back to that specific alignment. I was at a chambered tomb at Altwark, to the southeast of Arbor Low. The major axis of the tomb ran directly towards Arbor Low, but I could not find an energy ley there. I wondered if I could dowse the builders' intent to align the tomb with the marvelous recumbent stone circle, and sure enough, I found a 3 feet (1 m) wide line of intent going off to the northwest, towards Arbor Low. In effect, you could say I was dowsing a 4,000-year-old thought form.

One exercise that you can try is to have a friend place a thought form somewhere in a room. Your friend must be prepared to focus clearly, and

117

then not fool around once he or she has put the form in place. The form can be anything at all, from a single numeral to a complex colored image. You can try to dowse for where it is when your friend says the thought form is there. If you're careful, you can even dowse the shape of the form. Is it a pyramid? A cube? A sphere? Some other shape? See if you can 'feel' it with your hands.

I would suggest that if you want to dowse for thought forms, be sure to erase them when you're done. This can be done simply by waving your hand over them as if you were erasing a blackboard. This gesture focuses your intention to remove the form you have just made. Otherwise you may encounter the form when you are trying to find something else.

Thoughts, the emanations of our mind, are just as real as this book that you are now holding in your hand. I've placed a thought form of, and an actual triangle, on one of the squares of the World Map Chart (page 44). Can you find it? The thought form triangle and the drawn triangle form a Star of David (a six pointed star made from two equilateral triangles). Can you dowse the entire star? Check your answer on page 126.

DEVICELESS DOWSING

There are some dowsers who don't use tools like pendulums or Y rods, or even charts. They work without tools, and are called deviceless dowsers. In a sense, they have developed ways to always have their tools with them, but internally. This opens up a realm of topics which is really beyond the scope of this book. However, the following exercise suggests some easy ways to get started in this direction, if you want to.

Read this next paragraph and then put the book down and try this exercise. Do you know the screen on which you dream? The one between, and just above your eyes? On your screen, try to see your pendulum in the search position. Now see it move to yes and then no.

It might be easier to 'see' the movements if you keep your eyes open, but slightly out of focus. Don't look directly at anything, but 'see' the pendulum. My yes is clockwise, and my no is counterclockwise. I imagine the sign of Aries (♈) just above my eyebrows, and look at the point at the base where the two curves meet. I ask the question, and if I find my eyes going up and to the right, the answer is yes — up and to the left would be no. The trick, again, is to keep your conscious desire for a certain answer out of the process. Be aware of your need for a specific answer, but also make sure that need doesn't interfere with the Truth.

So many people today, who are products of a Western education, seem to be finding that there is something missing in their lives. In our search for Truth, the rational approach doesn't always seem to work, and more and more people are talking about new ways of intuitively knowing. This book is only the beginning. If you have found the pendulum useful, I urge you to find out more about this mercurial problem-solving device. I also urge you to join one of the organizations listed in the back of this book.

The pendulum, and the other tools described here, can help you to develop your intuition. They can help you in your own journey towards your Truth. Dowsing is certainly not the *only* way as some paths claim for themselves; however, more and more people are finding that dowsing is a balanced and useful tool in their lives. I hope you will join us.

BOOKS TO READ

Archdale, F.A. *Elementary Radiesthesia & The Use Of the Pendulum*. Health Research, Mokelumne Hill, California 1961 (available at ASD Book & Supply. Good beginning pamphlet.)

Bible, Revised Standard Version. Thomas Nelson & Sons, New York, 1959 (Dowsing and sacred geometry source book.)

Bird, Christopher. *The Divining Hand*, E.P. Dutton, New York, 1979 (History of dowsing in the last five hundred years.)

Graves, Tom. *The Diviner's Handbook*, Aquarian Press, Wellingborough, Northamptonshire, 1986 (Published in the US by Inner Traditions International Ltd., Rochester, Vermont, 1986.)

Graves, Tom. *Needles Of Stone Revisited*, Gothic Image Publications, Glastonbury, Somerset, 1986. Distributed in the US by The Great Tradition. (Dowsing and Earth Mysteries.)

Graves, Tom. *The Elements Of Pendulum Dowsing*, Element Books, Shaftesbury, Dorset, 1989

Graves, Tom. *The Dowsers Workbook*, Aquarian Press, Wellingborough, Northamptonshire 1989 (Published in the US by Sterling Publishing, New York, 1989)

Farrelly, Frances. *Search: A Manual of Experiments*, ASD Book & Supply, Danville, Vermont, 1988 (Map dowsing, ESP, psi workbook.)

Howard-Gordon, Frances. *Glastonbury Maker Of Myths*, Gothic Image Publications, Glastonbury, Somerset, 1982. Distributed in the US by New Leaf. (The Legends of Glastonbury, a Pilgrimage Town.)

Hitchings, Francis. *Dowsing: The Psi Connection*, Anchor Books/Doubleday, Garden City, New York 1978 (Good overview of dowsing.)

Jenkins, Palden. *Living In Time*, Gateway Books, Bath, Somerset, 1987. Distributed in the US by New Leaf. (A fresh look at the basics of astrology.)

Lonegren, Sig. *Earth Mysteries Handbook: Wholistic Non-intrusive Data Gathering Techniques*, ASD Book & Supply, Danville, Vermont, 1985 (Sacred geometry, archaeoastronomy and dowsing.)

Lonegren, Sig. *Spiritual Dowsing*, Gothic Image Publications, Glastonbury, Somerset, 1986. Distributed by New Leaf Distributors on the East Coast, and by Great Traditions in California. (Dowsing – earth energies, ancient sacred sites, and healing.)

MacLean, Gordon. *Field Guide to Dowsing*, ASD Book & Supply, Danville, Vermont, 1980 (Basic dowsing.)

Postman, Neil & Charles Weingartner. *Teaching as a Subversive Activity*, Delacorte Press, New York, 1969 (A gnostic cry in public/secondary education.)

Parker, Derek & Julia. *The Compleat Astrologer*, Mitchell Beazley Ltd, London, 1971 and McGraw-Hill Book Company, New York, 1971 (The complete beginning astrology book.)

Sheldrake, Rupert. A New Science Of Life, Blonde & Briggs Ltd., London, 1981 (Morphogenetic fields & reality as a hologram.)

Sjöö, Monica, & Barbara Mor. The Great Cosmic Mother: Rediscovering the Religion Of the Earth, Harper & Row, San Francisco, 1987 (Story of the Earth Mother.)

Starhawk. Dreaming the Dark: Magic, Sex & Politics, Beacon Press, Boston, 1982 (Feminist view of witchcraft persecutions.)

Underwood, Guy. The Pattern Of the Past, Abelard-Schuman Ltd., New York, 1973 (first published in 1969). (Advanced Earth energy dowsing.)

Watkins, Alfred. The Old Straight Track, Abacus, London, 1974 (First published in 1925, it was the first British book on ley lines.)

Willey, Raymond C. Modern Dowsing, ASD Book & Supply, Danville, Vermont, 1976 (Basic dowsing.)

DOWSING RELATED
ORGANIZATIONS AND PUBLICATIONS

Australia

The Bach Flower Remedies, Martin & Pleasance Wholesale Pty. Ltd., PO Box 4, Collingwood, Vic. Australia 3066.

Australia Dowsers Society of NSW, c/o 17 Blenheim Street, Randwick NSW, Australia 2031.

Fountain Groups (see Great Britain, Fountain International. There are over twenty Fountain Groups in Australia. Write c/o the British address for further information.)

Southern Tasmania Dowsing Association, PO Box 101, Moonah, Tasmania, Australia 7009.

Canada

The Bach Flower Remedies, Ellon (Bach USA) Inc., PO Box 320, Woodmere, New York 11598 (USA & Canadian distributor).

The Canadian Society of Dowsers, Allan Jeffrey, 277 Talbot Crescent, New Market, Ontario L3Y 1A4, Canada. (For membership and information.)

The Canadian Society of Questers, Donn McRae, Suite 200–8566 Fraser Street, Vancouver, British Columbia, V5X 3Y3, Canada.

Great Britain

Bach Flower Remedies Ltd., Dr. Edward Bach Centre, Mount Vernon, Sotwell, Wallingford, Oxon., OX10 0PZ England, (send for 'Bach Flower Remedies' pamphlet. Also dowsing chart, 'The Bach Flower Remedies, Natural Healing Chart').

The British Society of Dowsers, Sycamore Cottage, Tamley Lane, Hastingleigh, Ashford, Kent TN25, England.

OakDragon, Myrtle, Capel Seion Road, Drefach, Llanelli, Dyfed, Wales. Phone: (0269) 944272 (Wholistic outdoor camps that study various aspects of the Earth Mysteries.)

Fountain International, PO Box 915, Seaford, East Sussex BN25 1TW, England. (Fine magazine that many times includes articles on dowsing. Local Fountain Groups meet regularly.)

New Zealand

New Zealand Society of Dowsers, PO Box 41–095, St. Luke's, Mt. Albert, Auckland 3, New Zealand.

The United States Of America

The American Society of Dowsers, Danville, Vermont 05828. Phone (802) 684–3417. (Good basic and water dowsing classes. Local chapters around the country. Regional gatherings.)

ASD Book and Supply, Danville, Vermont 05828. Phone (802) 684–3417. (A good source for any books on dowsing and related subjects. Send for a catalog.)

The Bach Flower Remedies, Ellon (Bach USA)

Inc., PO Box 320, Woodmere, New York 11598 USA.

The Flower Essence Society, PO Box 459, Nevada City, California 95959.

Fountain Group. Cat Pettit, 502 Byrnes, San Antonio, Texas. Also, Johnathan Lane, 4694 1/2 30th Street, San Diego, California 92116.

New England Antiquities Research Association (NEARA), c/o Betty Lewis, 172 Robin Hill Road, Chelmsford, Massachusetts 01824. (Ancient sites in New England. Very open to dowsing. Membership $20.00 a year.)

OakDragon, Box 218, Greensboro, Vermont 05841. Phone (802) 533–2240. (Information about OakDragon gatherings.)

West Germany

The Bach Flower Remedies, Bach Centre German Office, Eppendorfer Landstr. 32, 2000 Hamburg 20, West Germany.

Boden Mensch Wetter, Dr. E. Hartmann, Editor, Adolf Knecht Strasse 25, D–693 Eberbach, West Germany.

Fountain Group, c/o Dr. Jantach, Isengaustrasse 21, 8000 Munich 83, West Germany.

Zeitschrift fur Radiesthesie, W. Wentzel, Editor, Kirchbachweg 16, Herald Bergal, 8 Munich 71, West Germany.

INDEX

WORLD MAP CHART

The answers to the map dowsing exercise on pages 44/45 are expressed as grid coordinates. Look for the coordinate you have dowsed and if it is here, you have struck oil! If it is not listed, go back and dowse the World Map Chart again.

A1, B1, B2, C1, C2, C4, C5, D1, D2, D3, D4, D5, D6, D7, E2, E3, E4, E5, E6, E7, F1, F4, F5, F6, F7, F8, F9, F10, G2, G3, G4, G7, G8, G10, G11, G12, G13, H2, H4, H8, H11, H12, H13, I9, I10, I11, J2, K1, K2, K4, K5, K6, K7, K8, L2, L3, L4, L5, L8, M1, M2, M3, M4, M5, M9, M10, M11, N1, N4, N5, N6, O1, O3, O4, O5, O6, O8, O9, O10, O11, P1, P5, P6, P7, P8, Q1, R1, R5, R7, S1, S3, S4, S6, T1, T2, T6, T7, T8, U1, U2, U3, U4, U5, U6, U7, U8, U9, U10, U11, V1, V2, V3, V4, V8, V9, V11, V12, W8, W9, W10, W12, X8, X9, X10, X12, X13, Z12.

The answer to the six-pointed star thought form exercise on page 118 is placed on the World Map Chart at coordinate L7.

THANK YOUS

I appreciate the initial help that Frances Howard-Gordon, Jamie George and Oliver Caldecott of Gothic Image in Glastonbury gave me when they introduced me to Ian Jackson and Nick Eddison, and Christine Moffat, my editor at Eddison Sadd Editions. There are many others who have helped shape this book in so many ways, and while I can't mention them all, I would particularly like to thank Linda Cameron, John Forward, Tom Graves, Sue Holmes, Kelly Hunter, Carol Irons, Donna Mackay, Steven Lawrence, my sister Sally Lonegren, Paul Sevigny, Joanna Trainor, and my children, Lucas and Jordan. I want to especially thank Eleanor Ott for all her work in reading the first draft of this book, and Palden Jenkins who helped me with the second draft.

Sig Lonegren can be reached at Box 218, Greensboro, Vermont, USA. Phone (802) 533 2240.

ACKNOWLEDGMENTS

Eddison Sadd Editions acknowledge contributions from the following people:

Creative Director *Nick Eddison*
Editorial Director *Ian Jackson*
Designer *Nigel Partridge*
Editor *Christine Moffat*
Indexer *Ailsa Allaby*
Illustrator *Vanessa Card*
Chart artworks *Anthony Duke, Dave Sexton*
Front box base photograph *Malkolm Warrington*
Front box photomontage *Copelands 24-hour-lab*
Production *Bob Towell*

ABOUT THE AUTHOR

Sig Lonegren has been a student of sacred enclosures since the late 1960s and he has a Masters degree in Sacred Space, the study of pre-Protestant Reformation spiritual centers. He is the author of the *Earth Mysteries Handbook: Wholistic Non-intrusive Data Gathering Techniques*, in which he discusses sacred geometry, archaeoastronomy and dowsing, and *Spiritual Dowsing*, a book that explores dowsing both as a tool for locating earth energies found at ancient sacred sites, and for health and healing. Sig is a past Trustee of the American Society of Dowsers, and was head of their Dowsing School for several years. While his home is in Vermont, USA, he spends time each year in the heart of King Arthur's Avalon, at Glastonbury, England. For the past four years Sig has been contributing to Earth Mystery gatherings with people in Britain. These week long encampments, put together by a group called OakDragon, focus on specific topics like music and dance, astrology, healing, creativity, ceremony, and the study of the experience of ancient Britain.